Dedicated my sons

Amando and Nathaniel,

this is a gift to let you know if you have a dream go for it.

Table of Content

I Am Your Canvas, You Are My Paint
Acrylic Brown
Anonymous
Art
Energy
Eyes Upon Eyes
I Like
Instructor
Lip Stick
Lost Book
Pose
Grab My Locs
Palette
Muse
Reminiscing
Www Dot Calm
Practice
Probabilities
Reflection
Quick Key
Speak
Waitress
Watch Me
Sound
No Where Too Far
Two, Three, Four Play
Beautiful Chaos
Abstract
Body of Lines
Dicktionary
Boston Mead
Delusion
Converse-Universe
Forty Thoughts
Love

What's My Inspiration?

Inspiration comes in many forms all rooted by that one thought.
Growing up I always was the shy kid, who never spoke.
When my mom introduced me to art, it helped me to communicate
in ways I didn't know how. Art helped me to realize I had a voice.
As a full time, artist, I had a hard time deciding which direction
I wanted to go in because I am the type of person who thinks
Non-Stop. One day I woke up and asked myself: "what inspires me?"
and the only word that came to mind was happiness.
Even though happiness comes in many forms; art is my happiness.
After committing to the thought, everything came into place, even
when I didn't understand it. As I continued to work towards my happiness,
things eventually made sense to me. During this time, I was living in
a new environment, I learned new things and gained confidence in
the art world. As of today, my art is currently displayed Internationally.
I accomplished this feat by pursuing my happiness. Along
my journey I have become a figure model for drawing sessions and a
live painter, which is painting live in front of an audience. Painting
live helped me see what inspires me. My art brings joy to familiar and
unfamiliar faces all over the world. This is a living inspiration for me.

Hope you enjoy my love with art. I always
say this "you can achieve whatever dreams
and goals you ever wanted to accomplish.
"ALL YOU HAVE TO DO IS PUT ACTION BEHIND IT.
" This is my dream and hope you enjoy my actions.

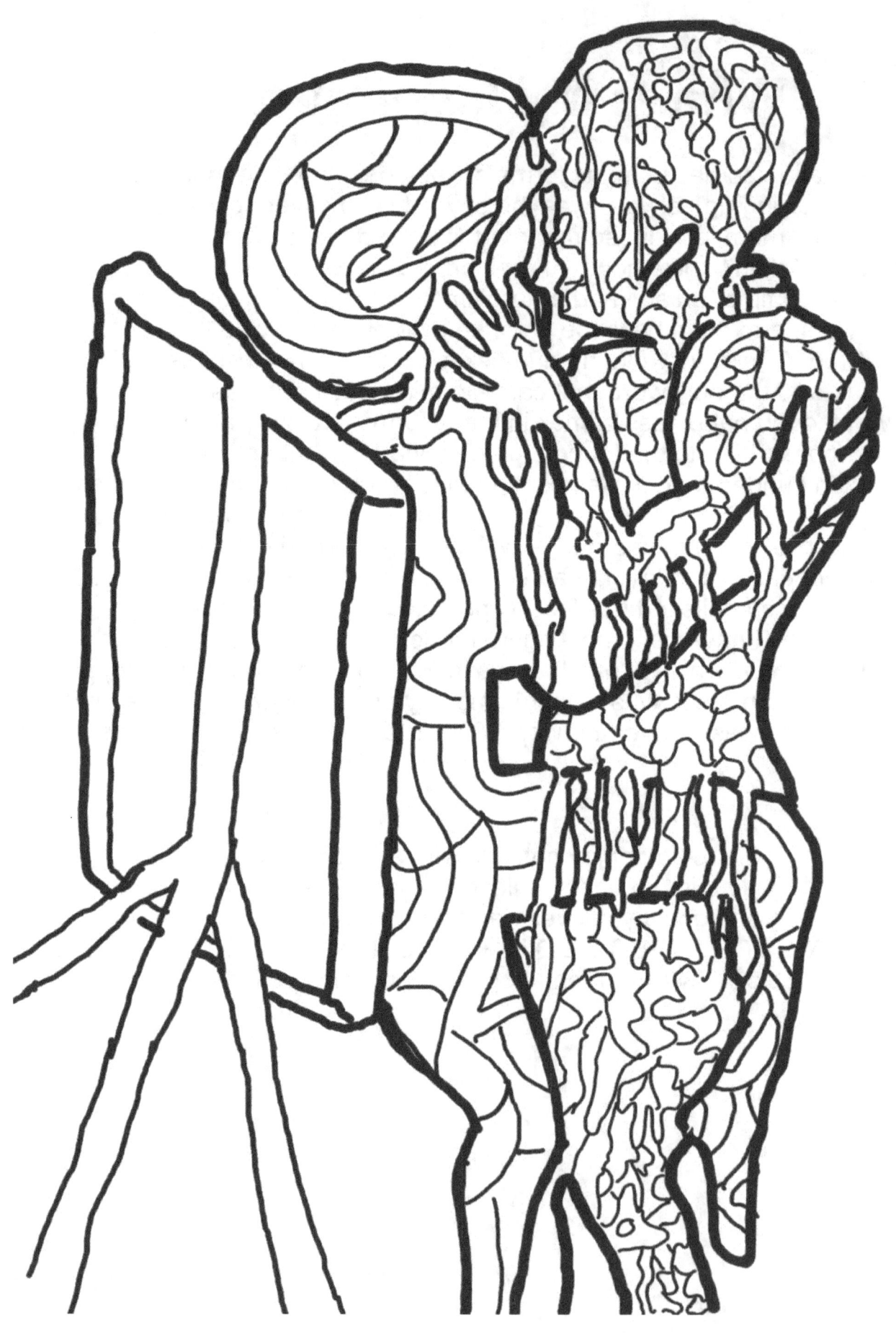

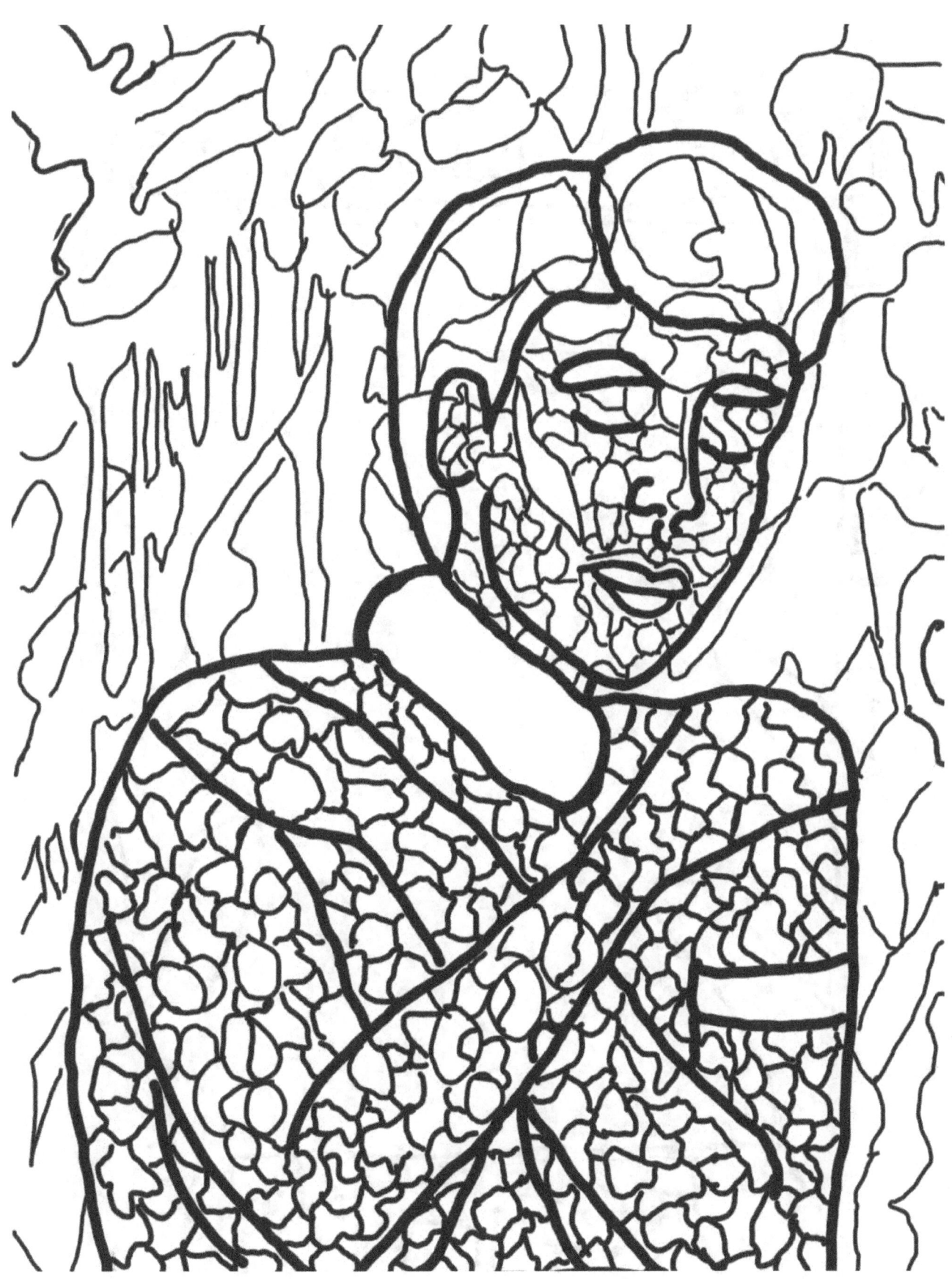

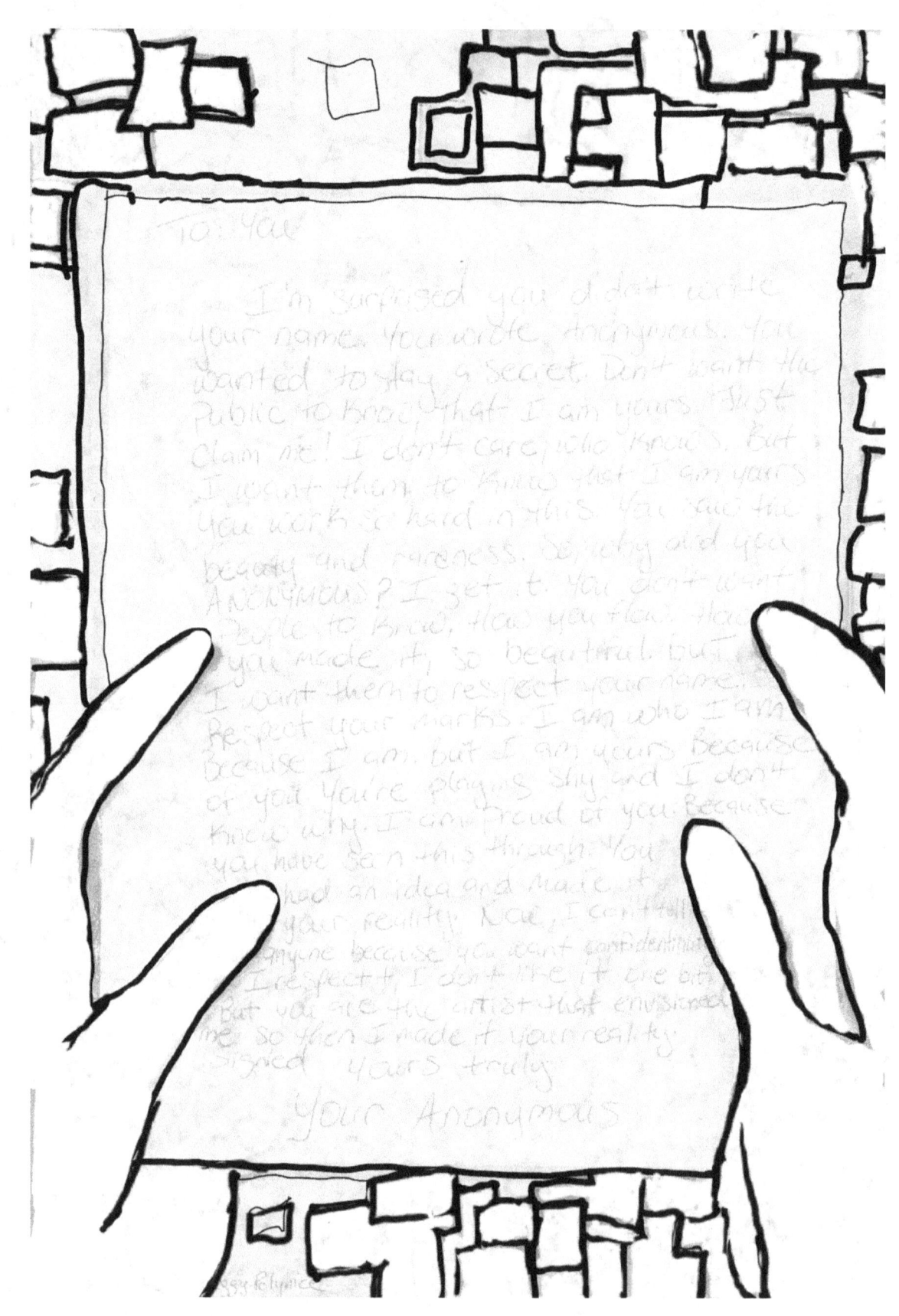

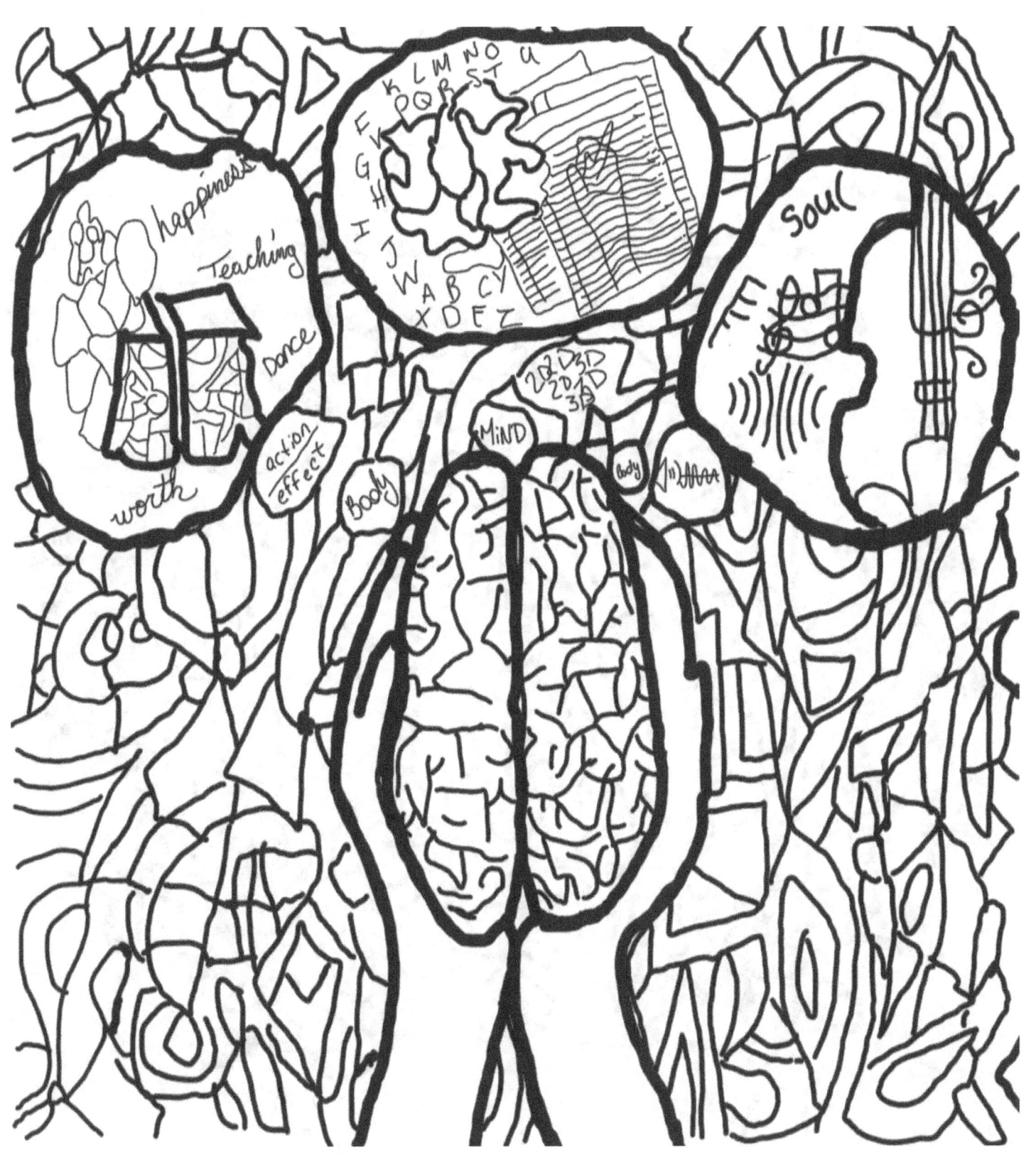

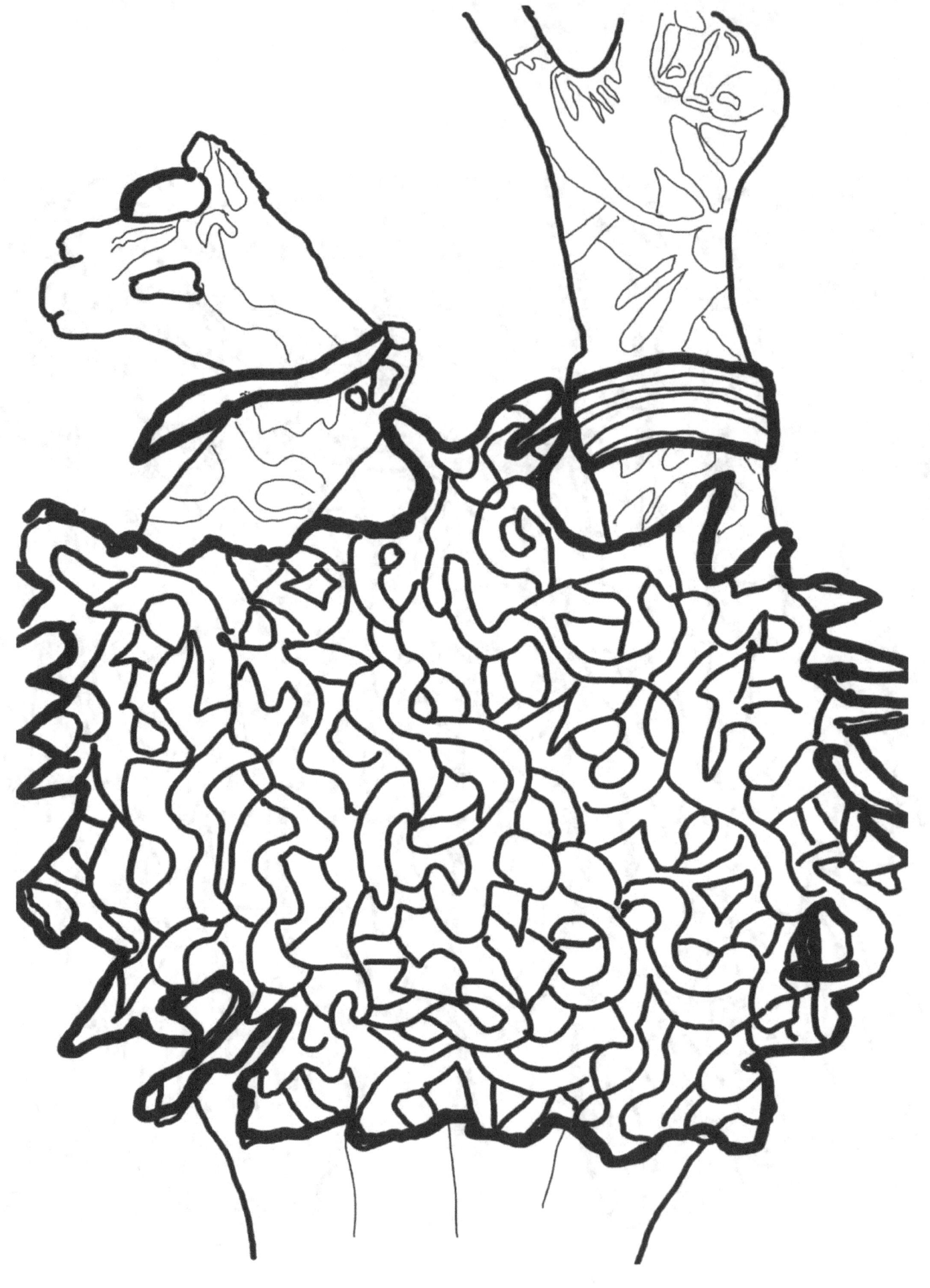

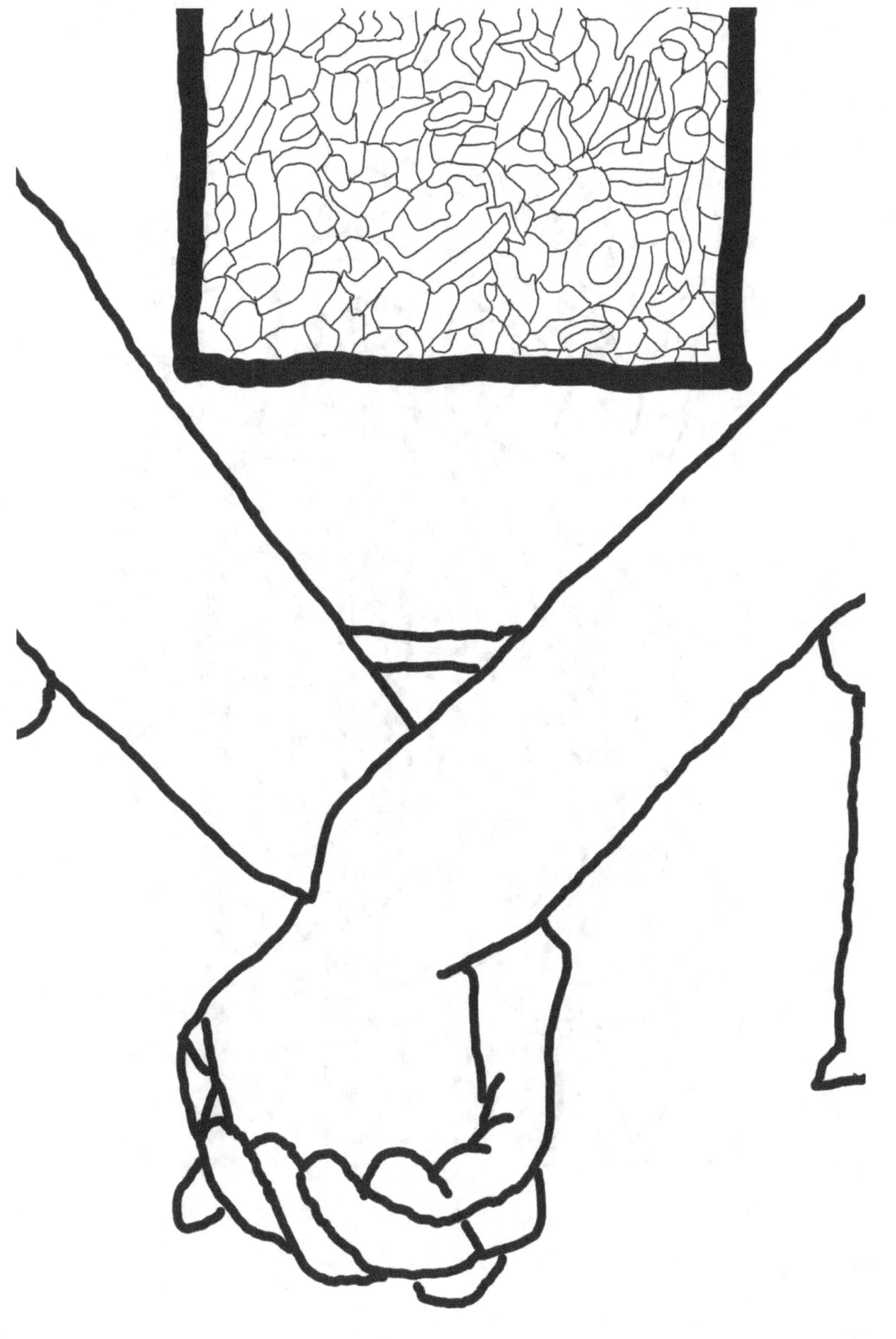

Turn on its side

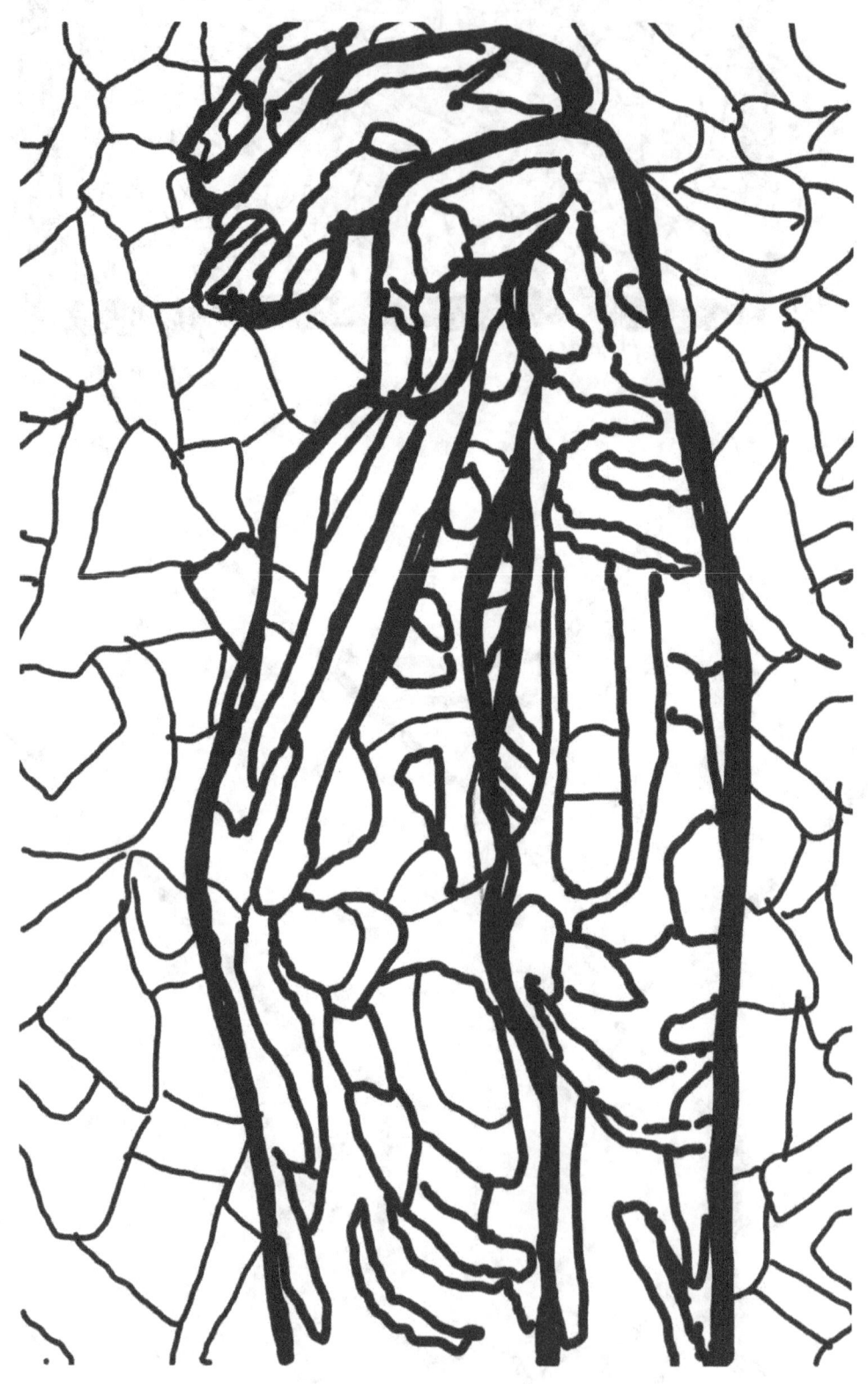

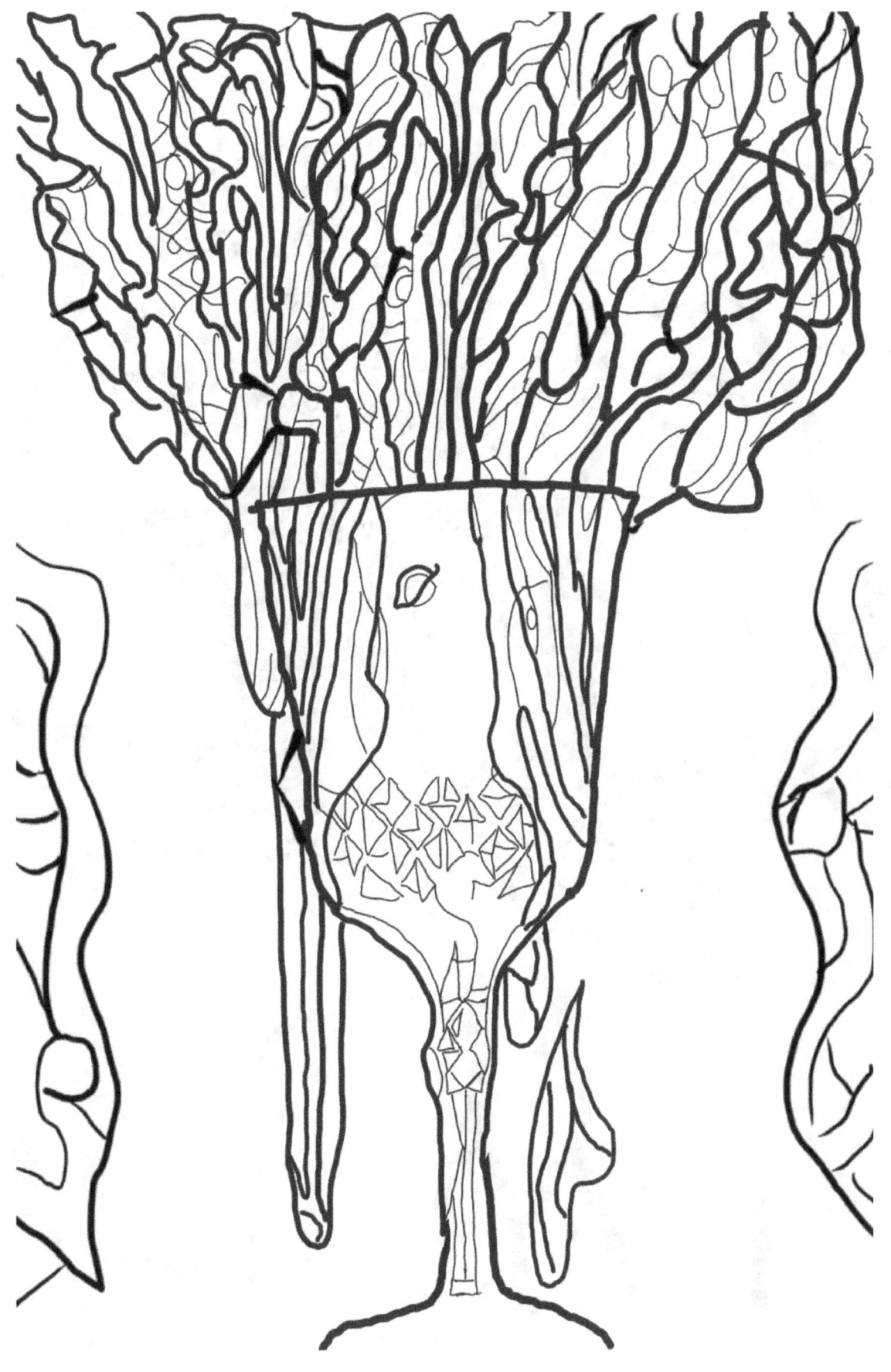

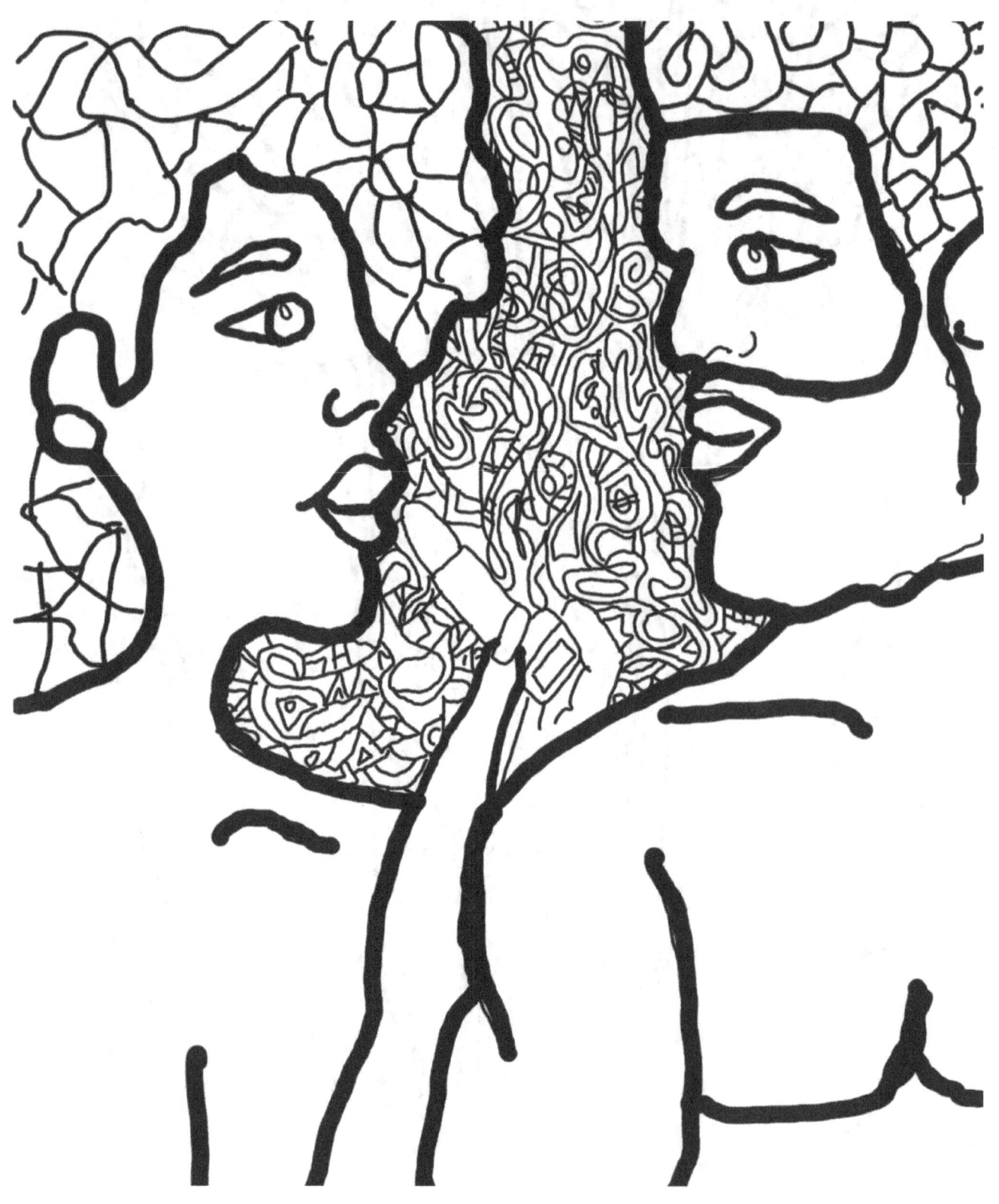

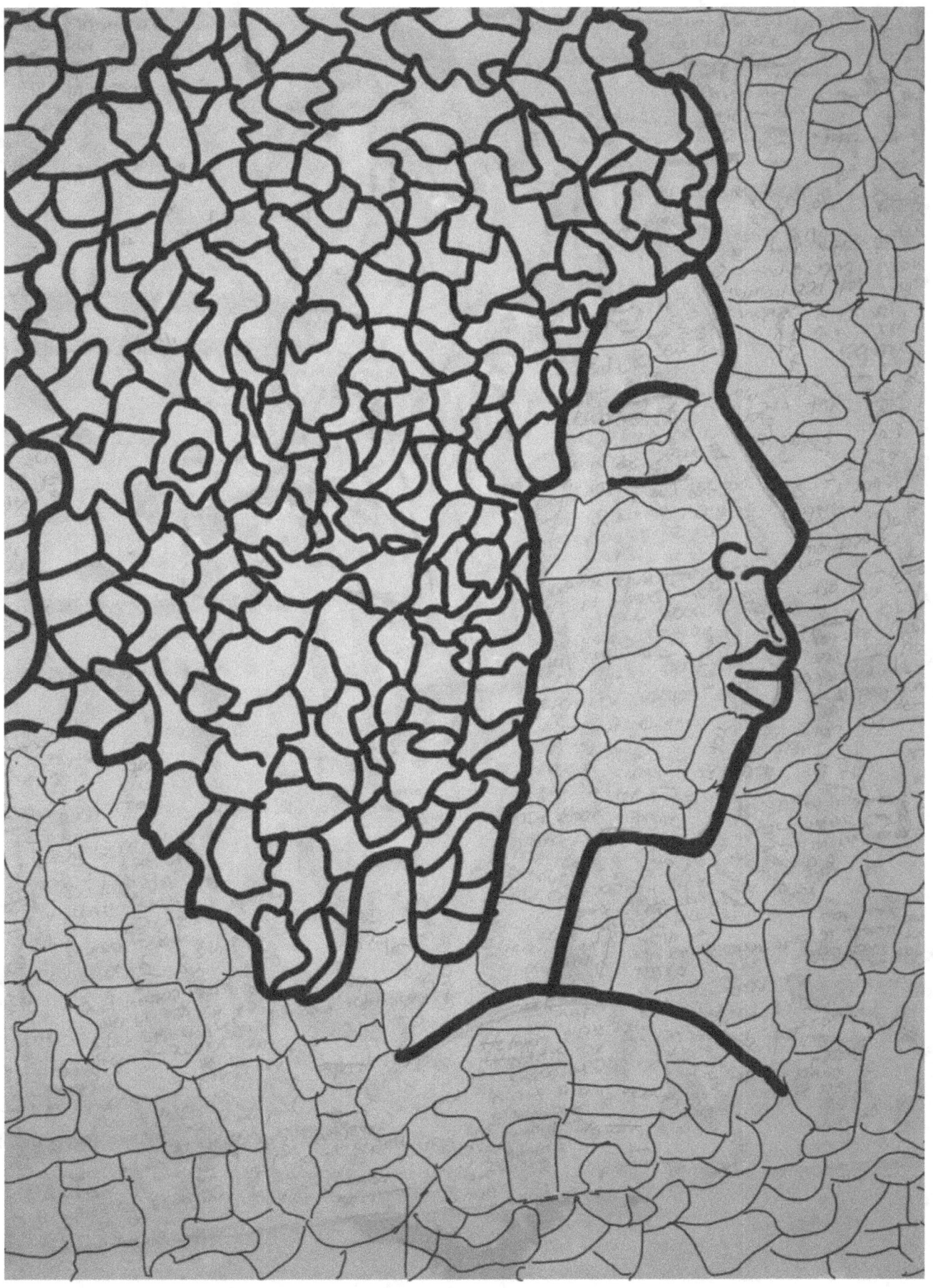

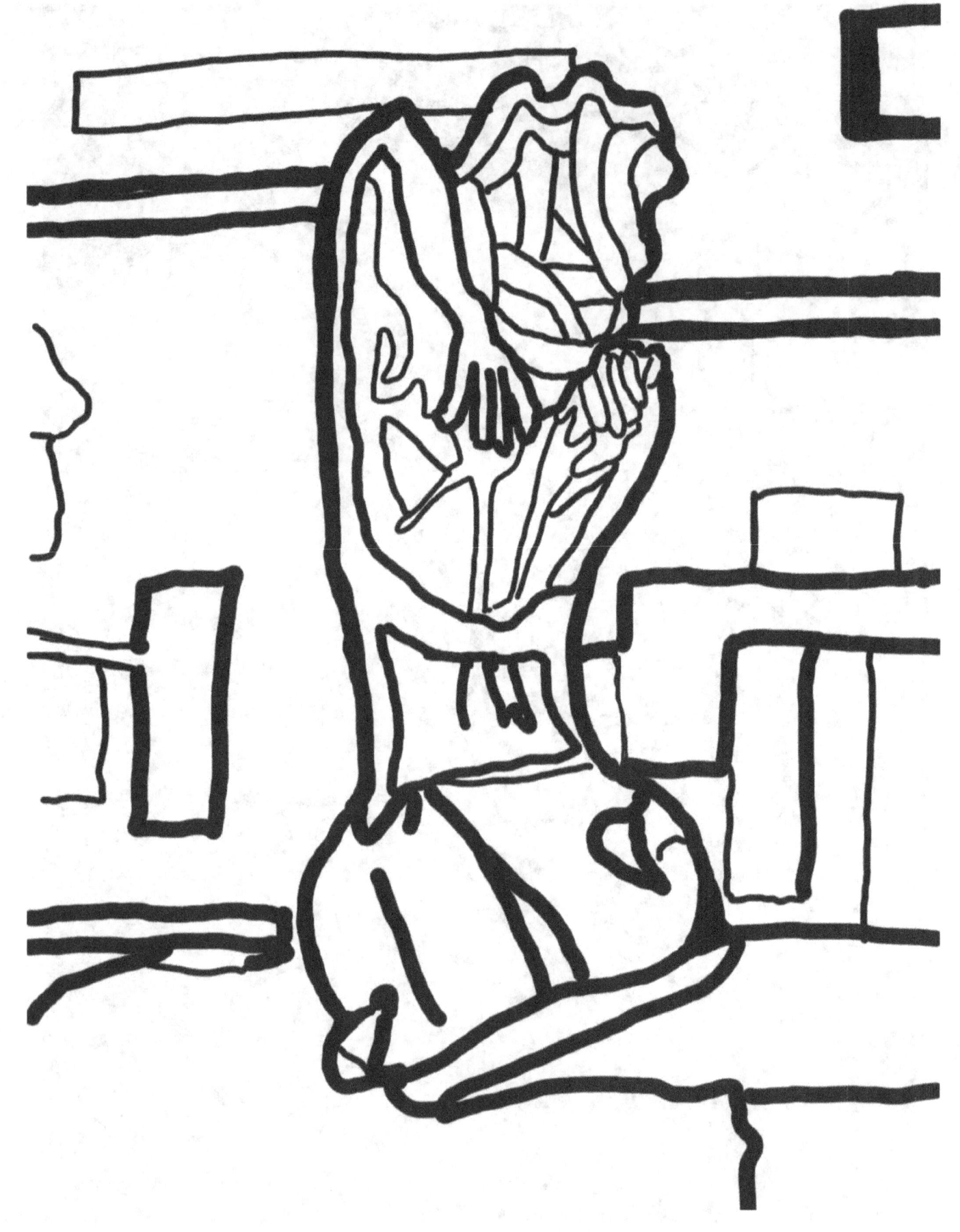

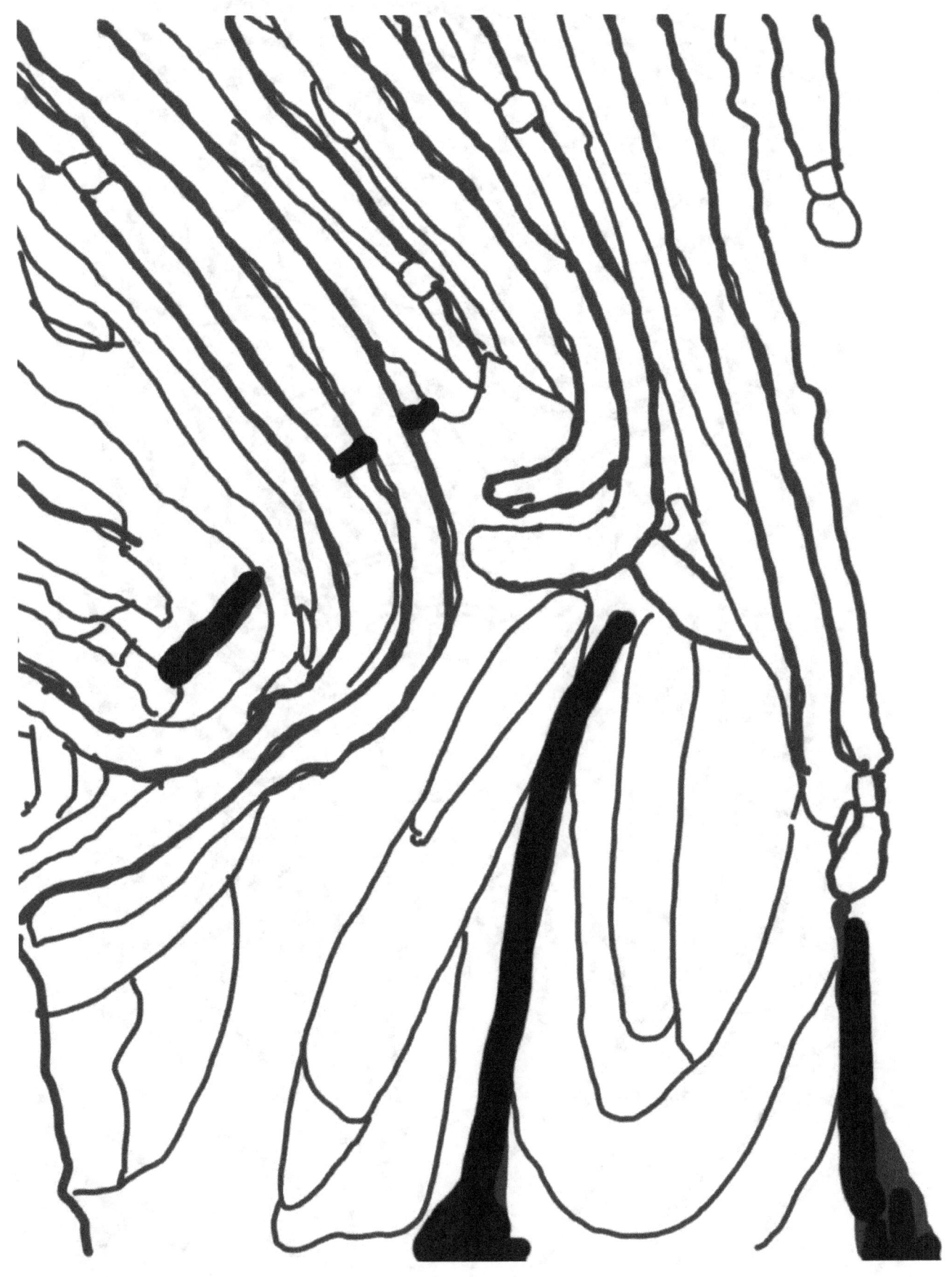

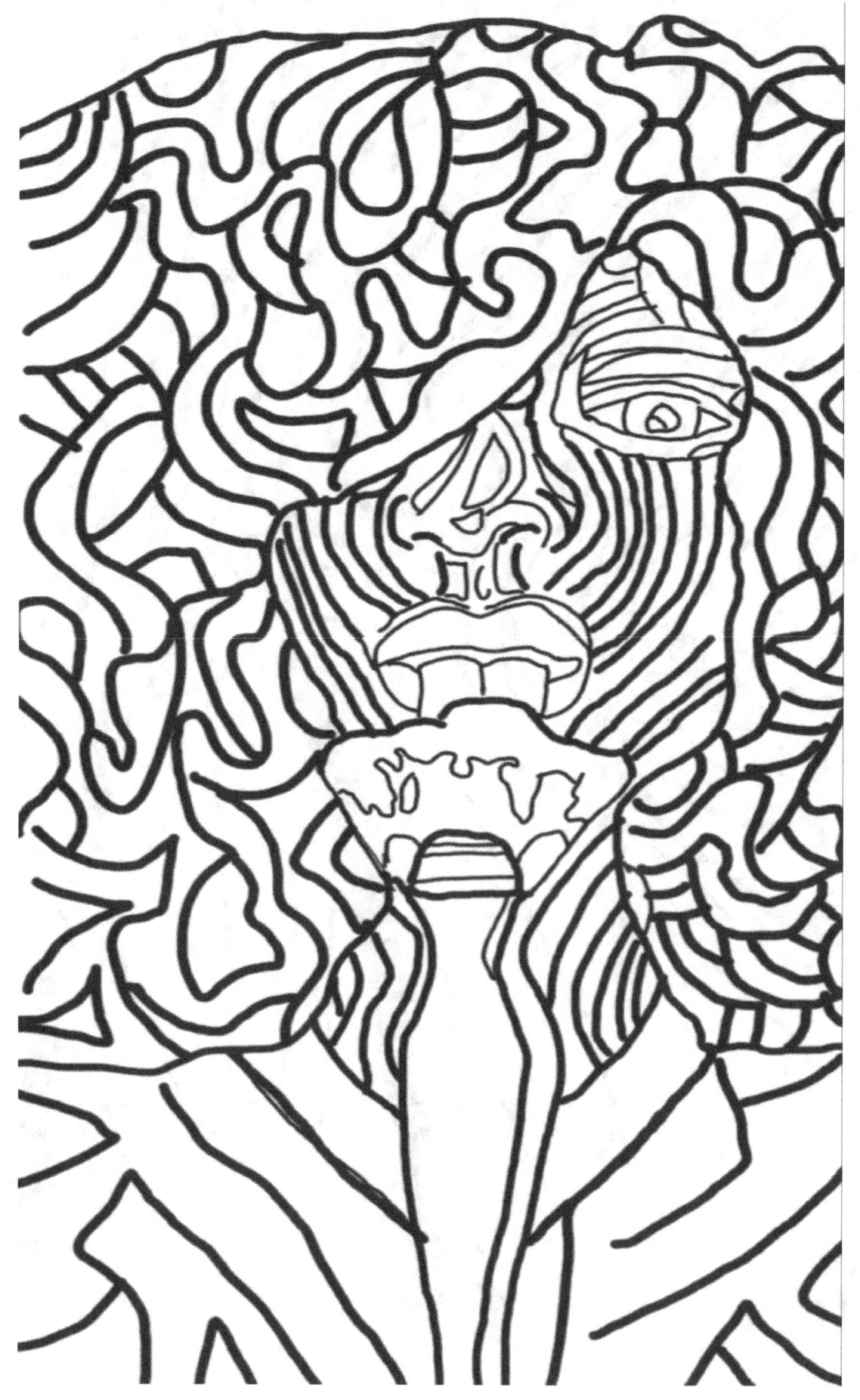

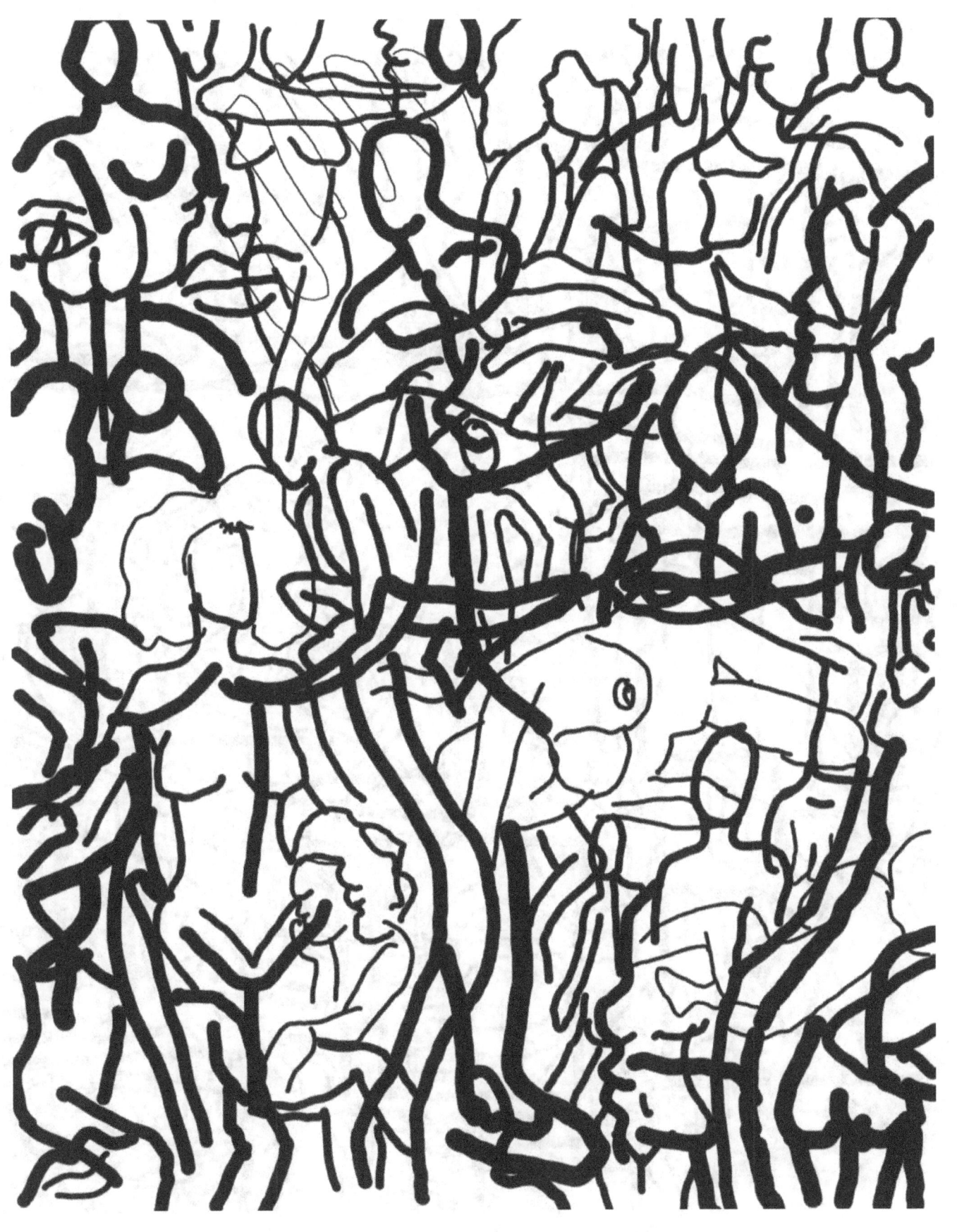

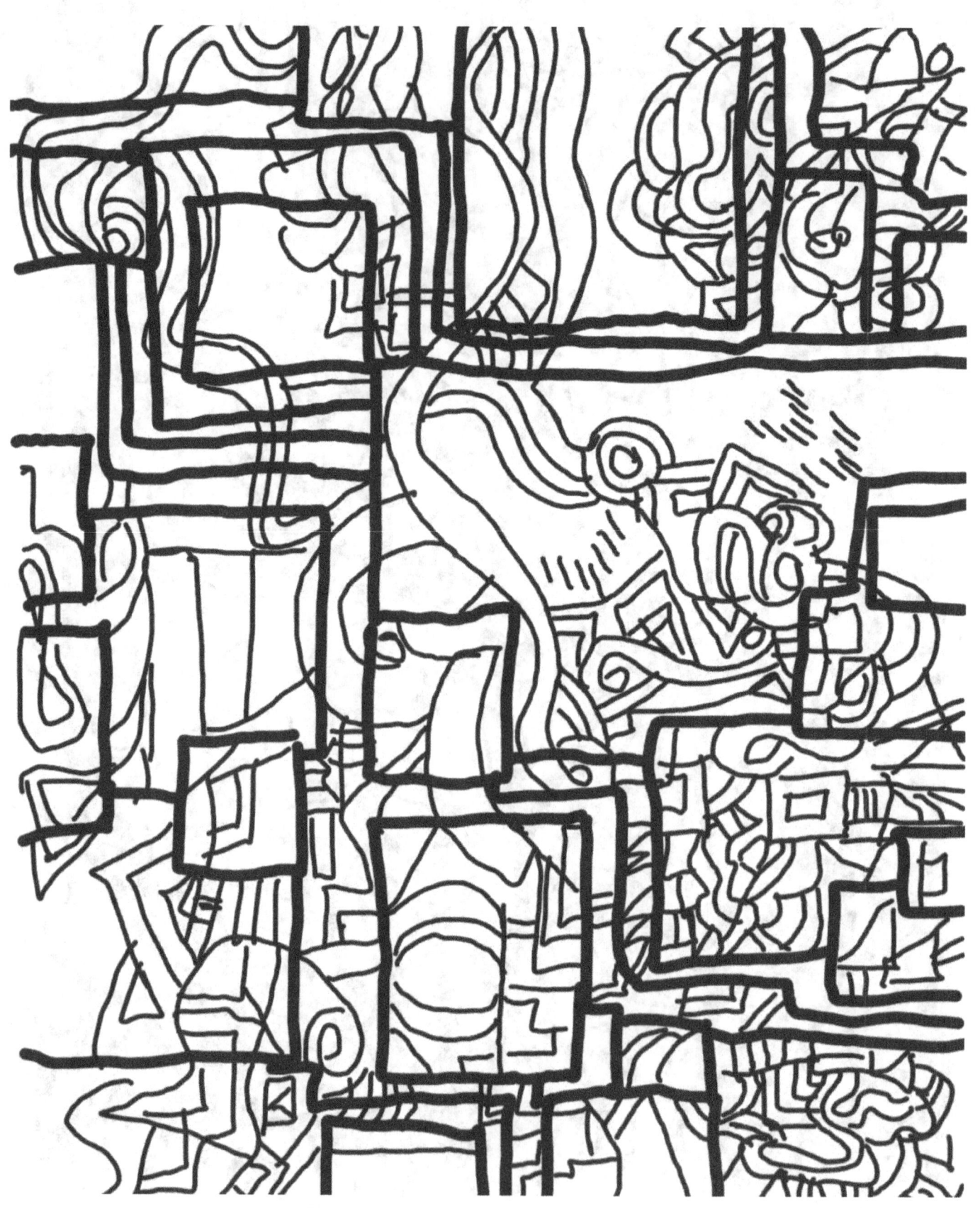

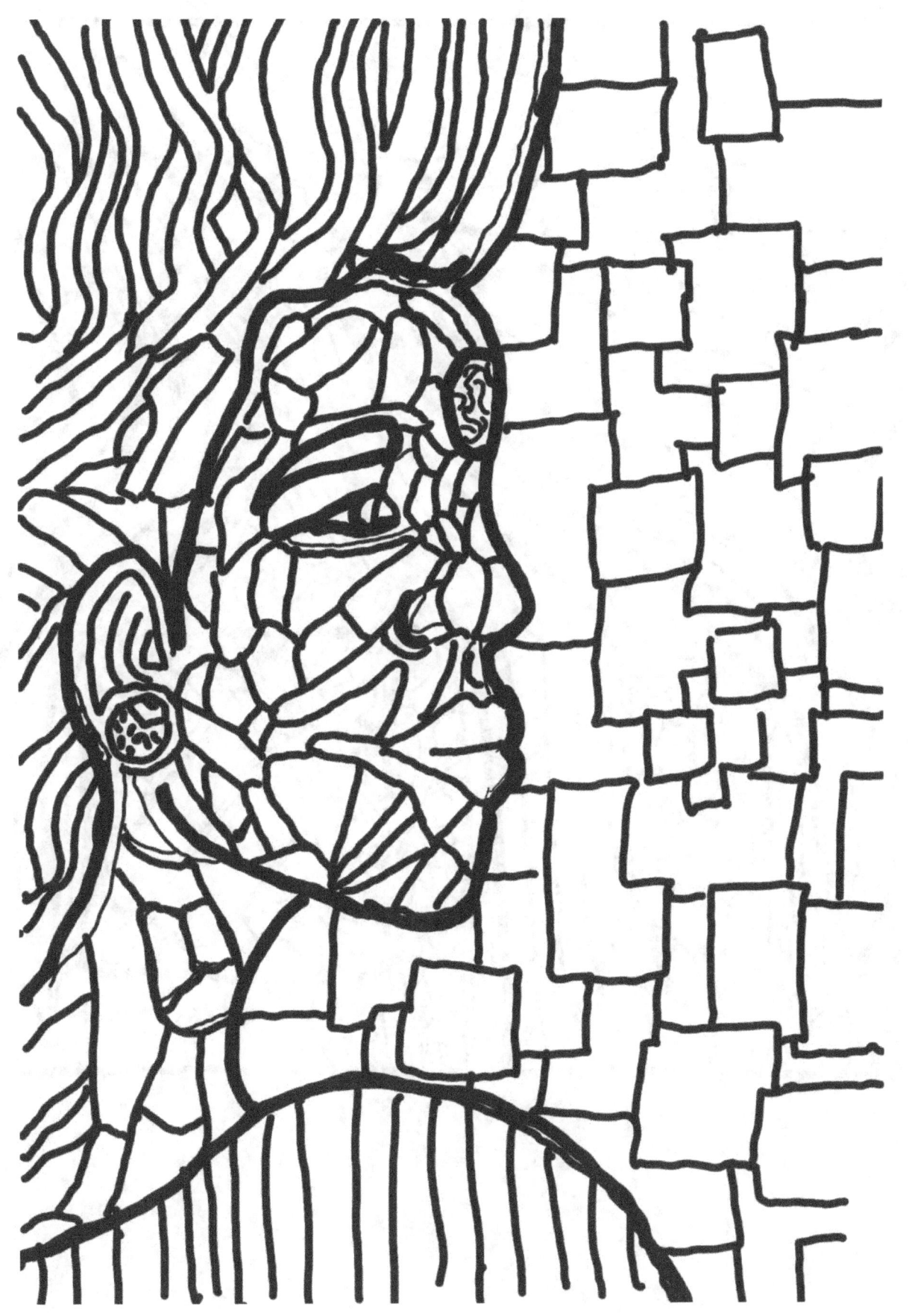

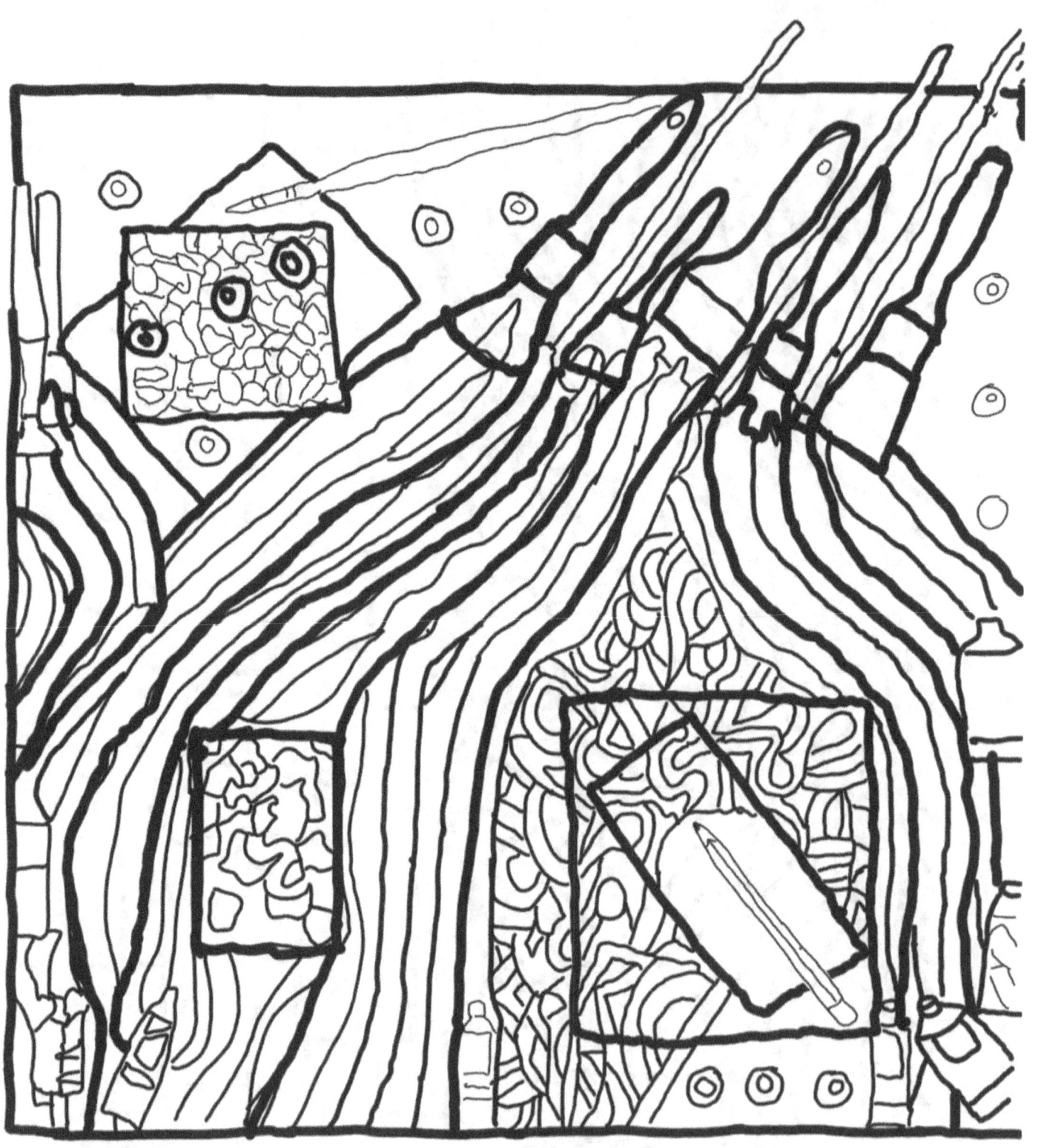

Turn on its side

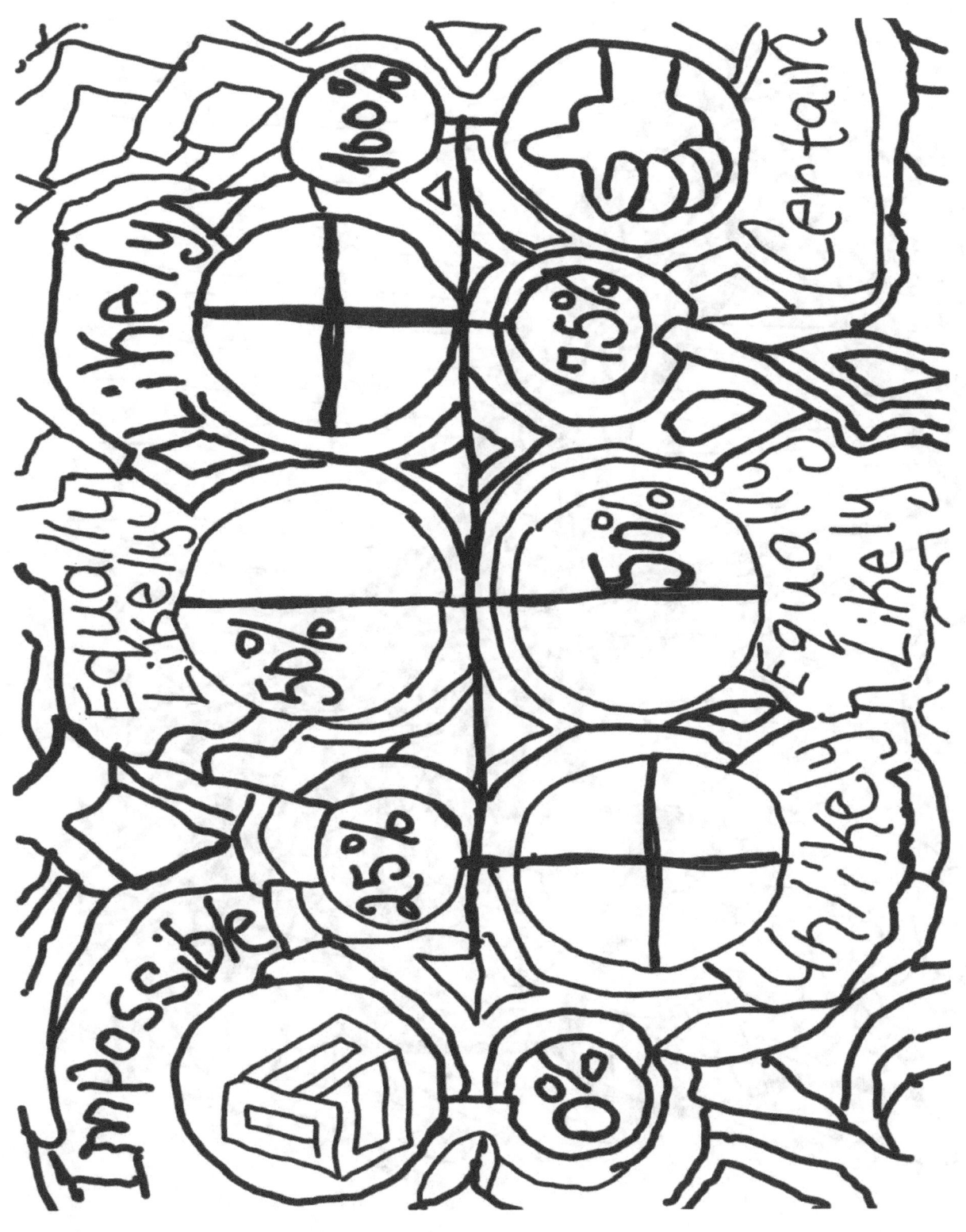

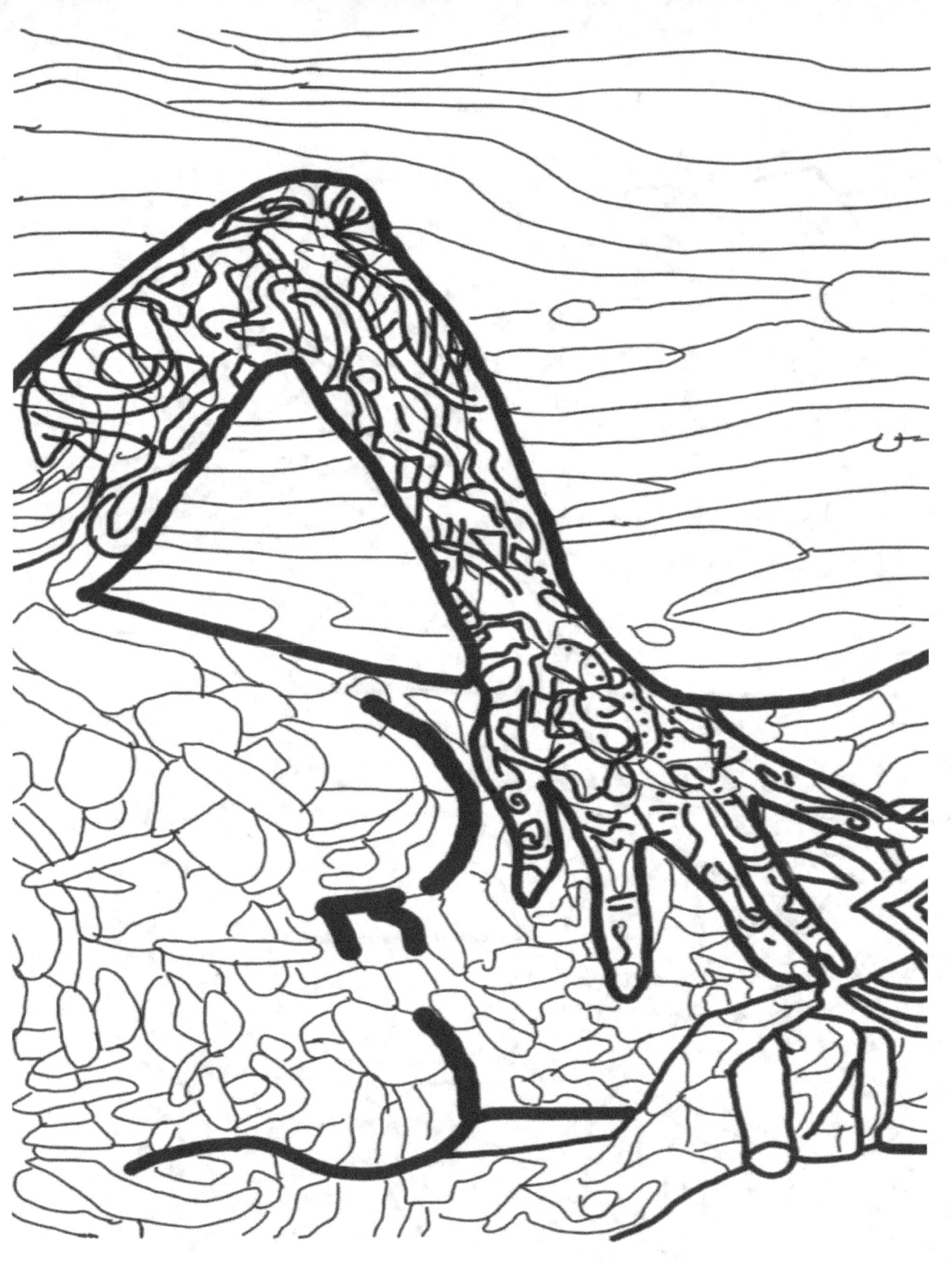

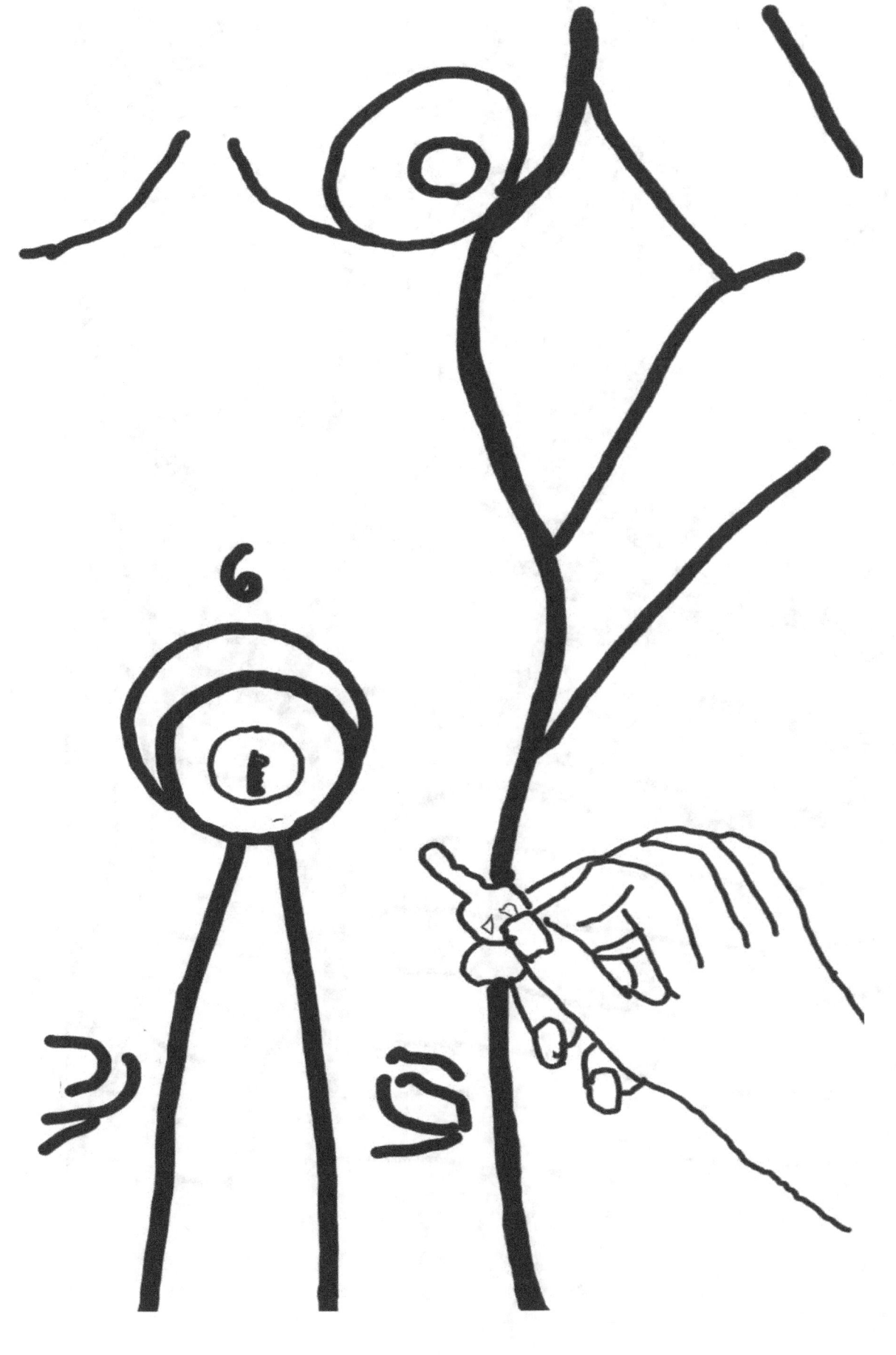

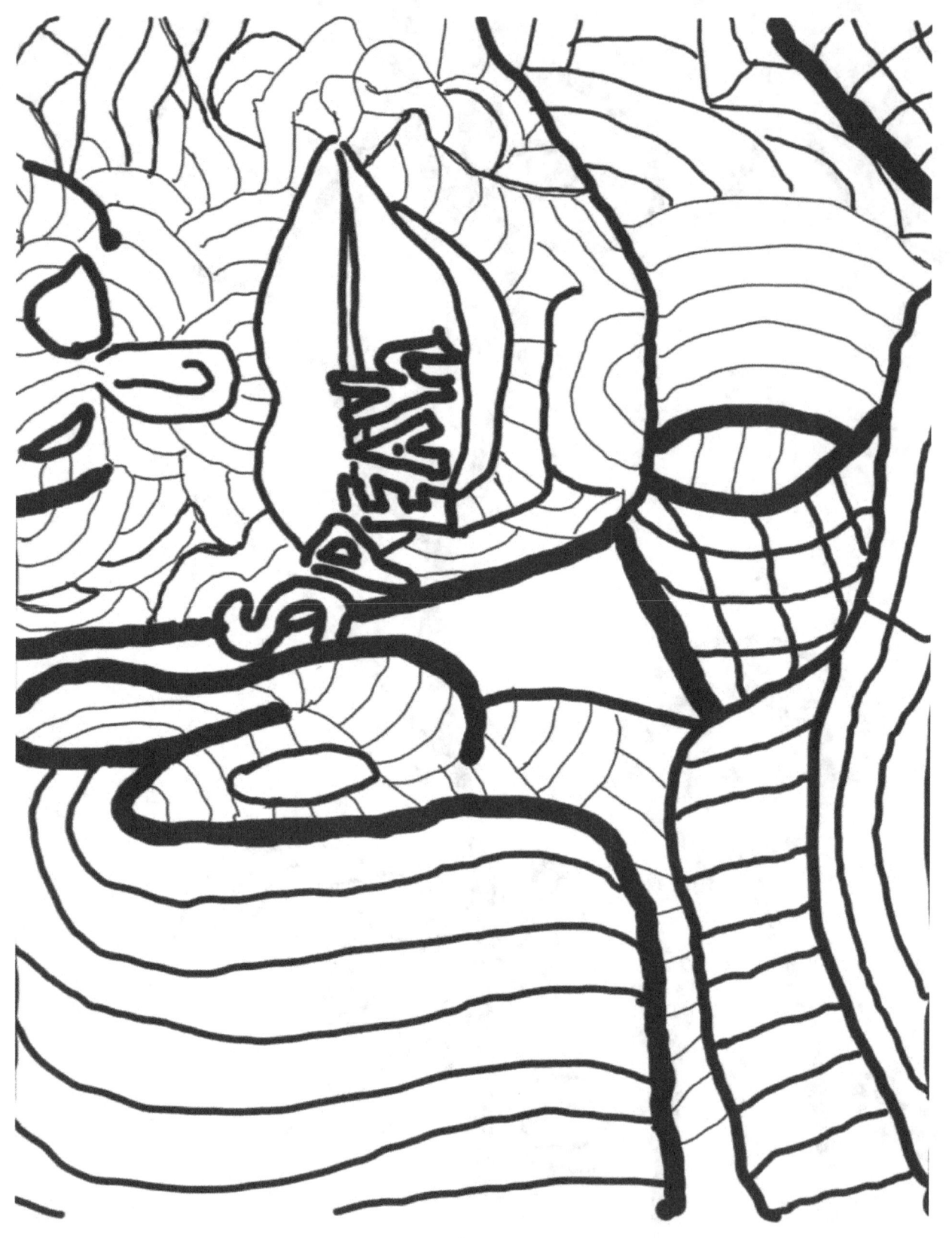

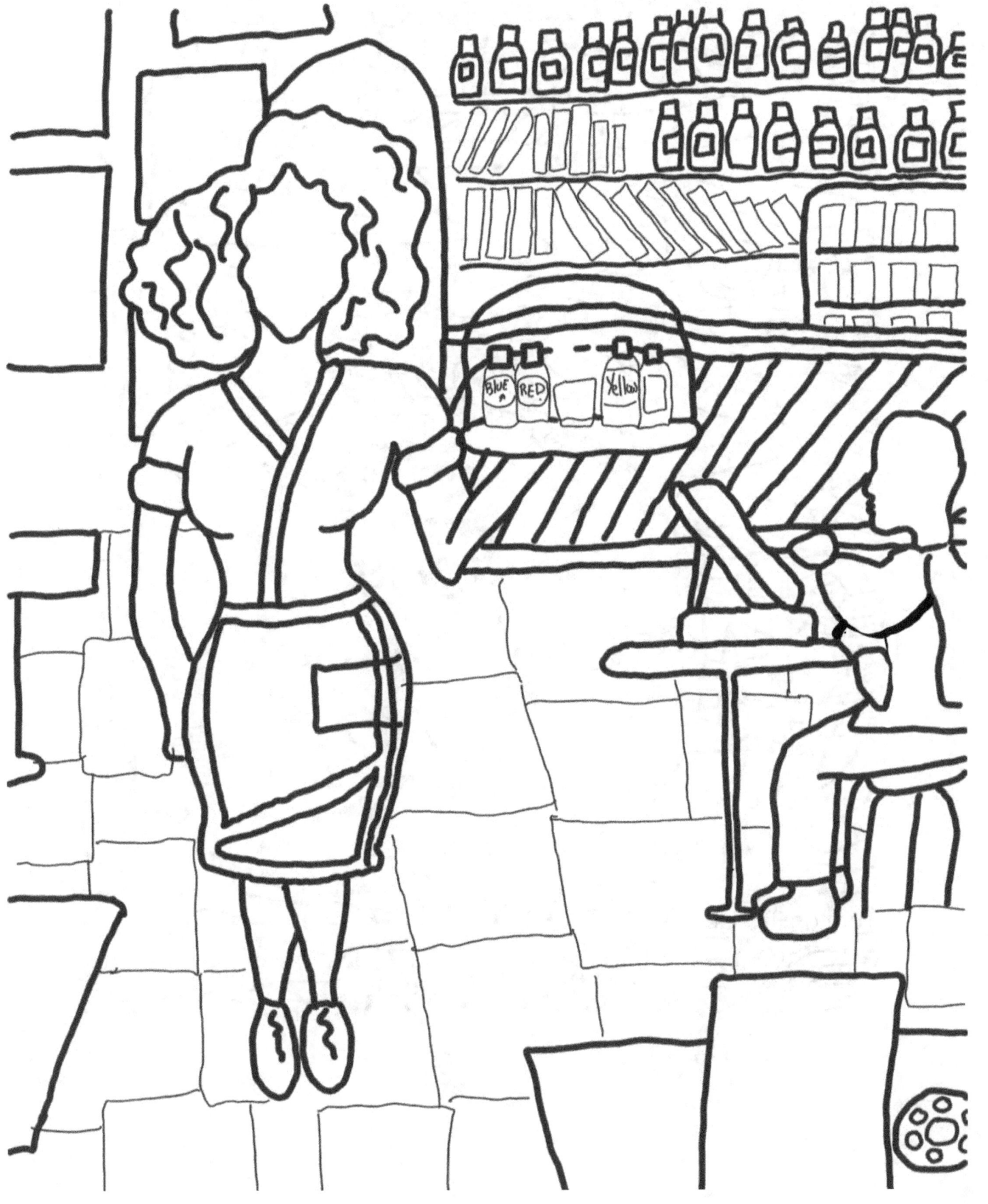

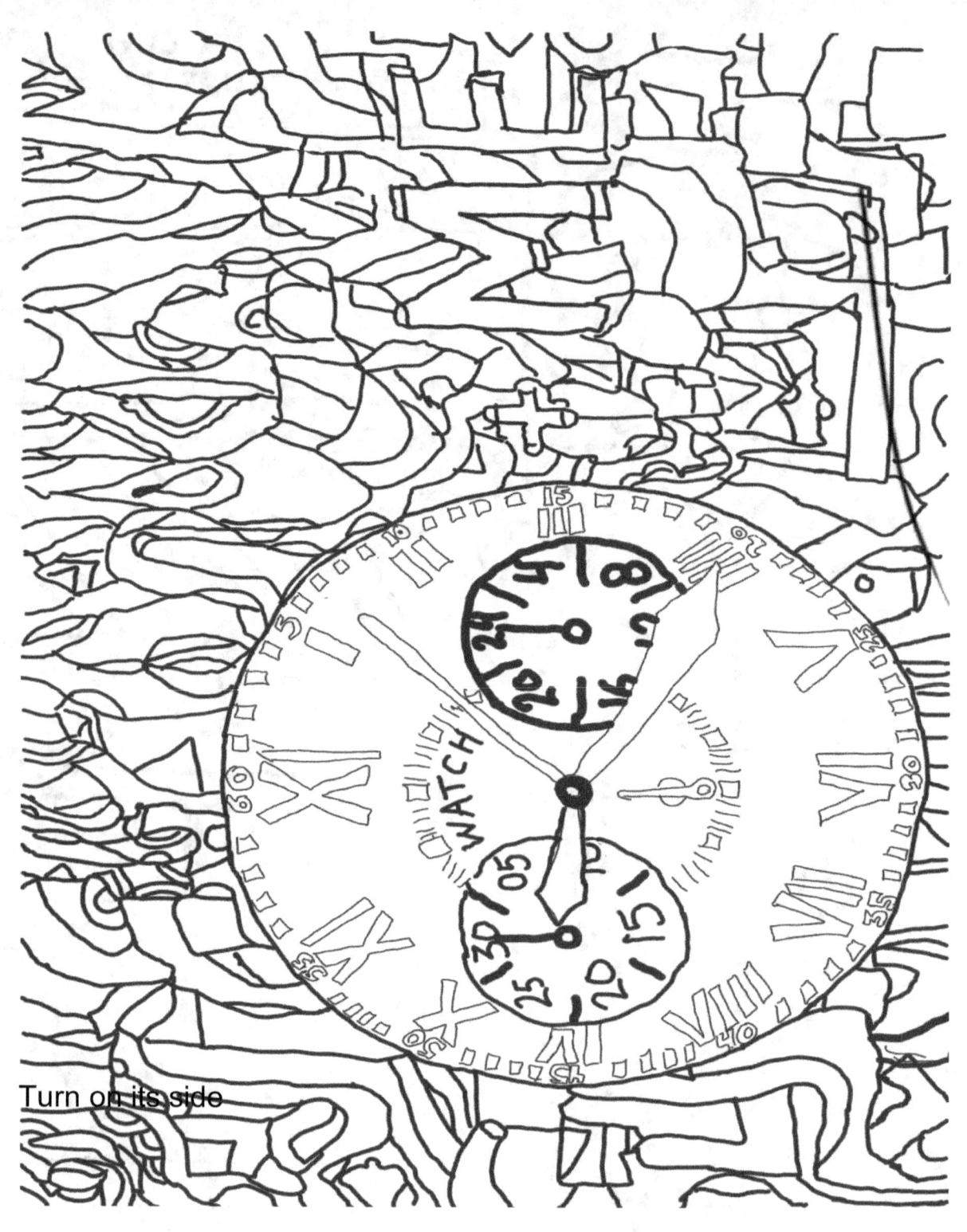

Turn on its side

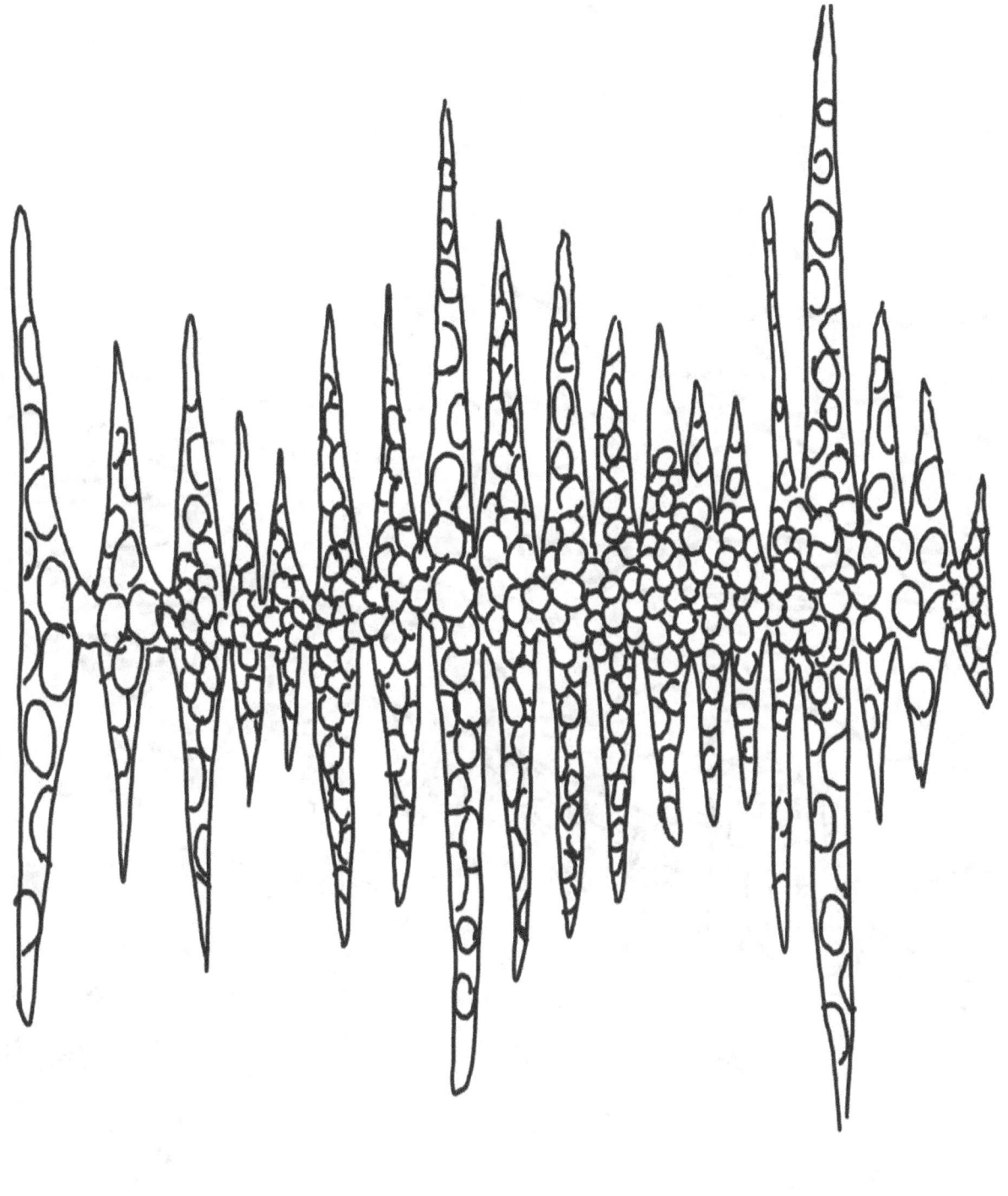

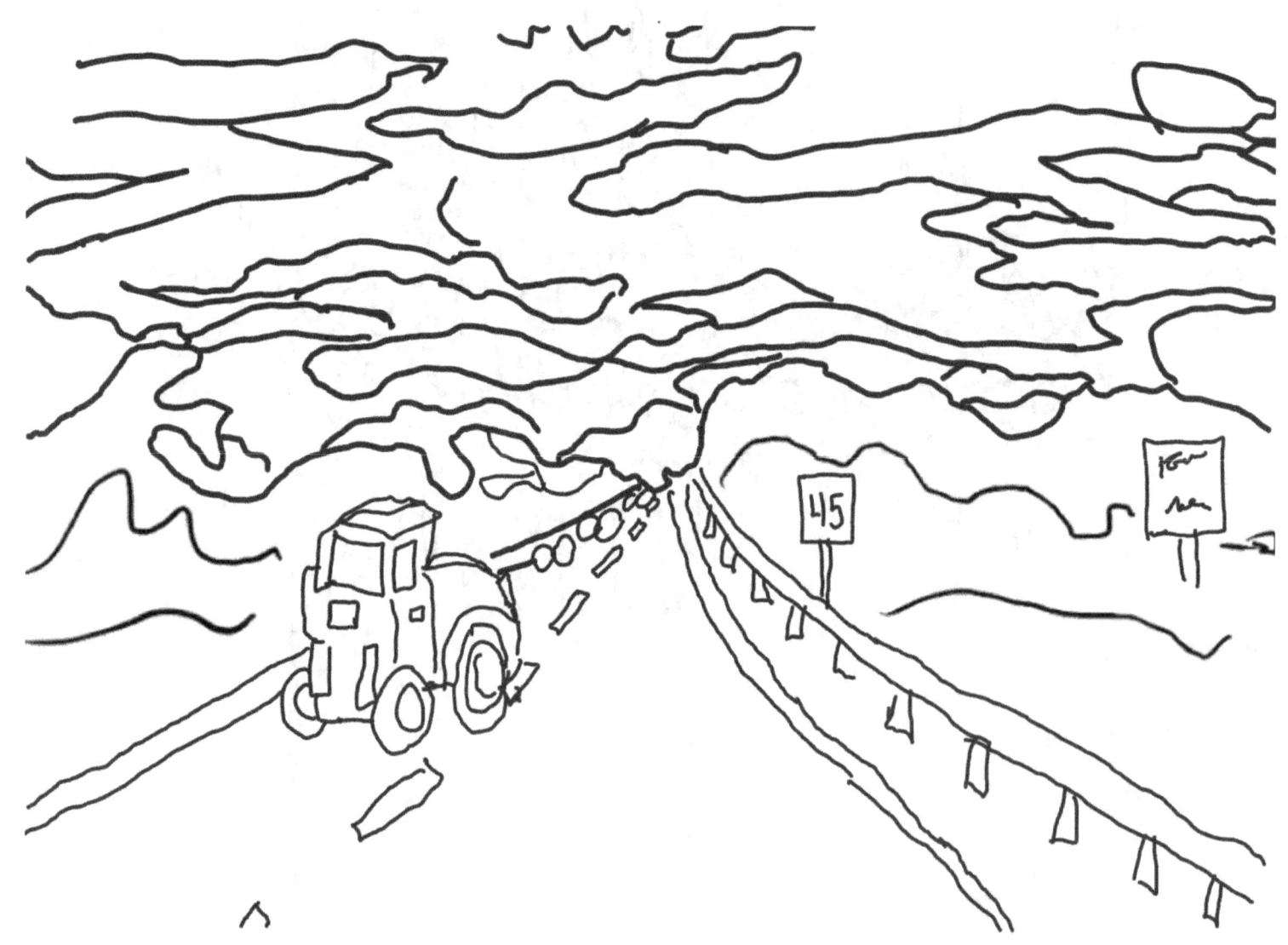

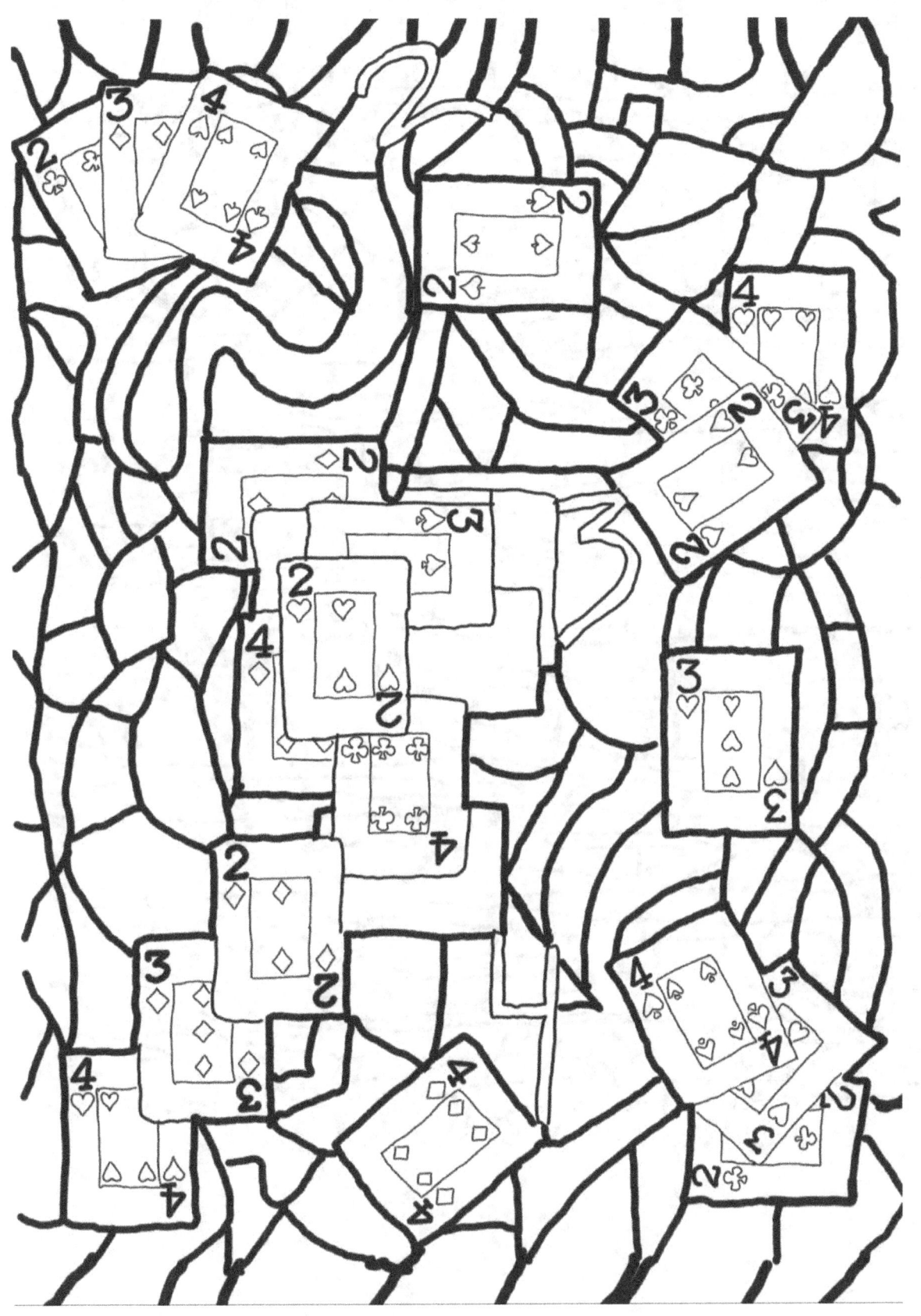

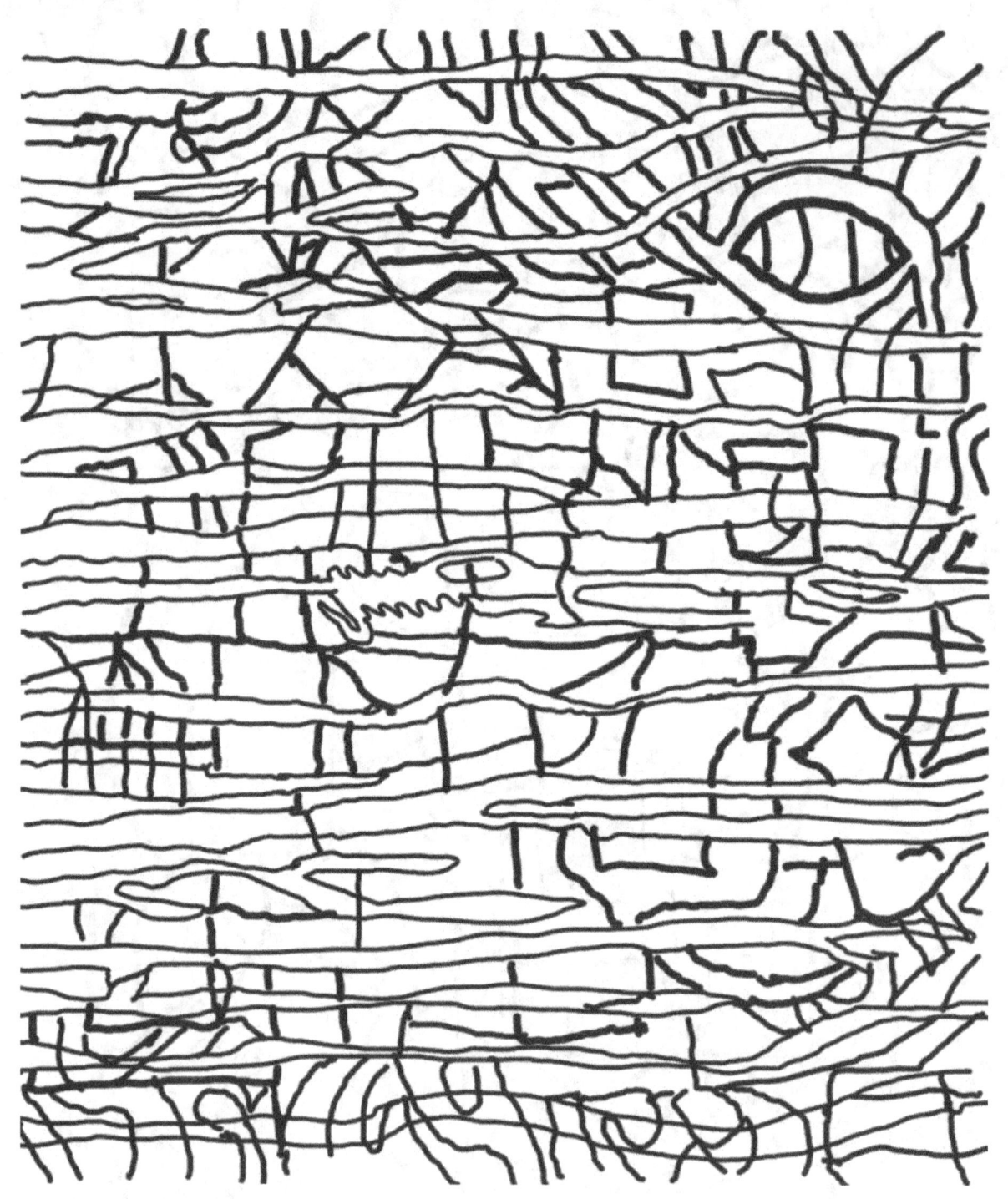

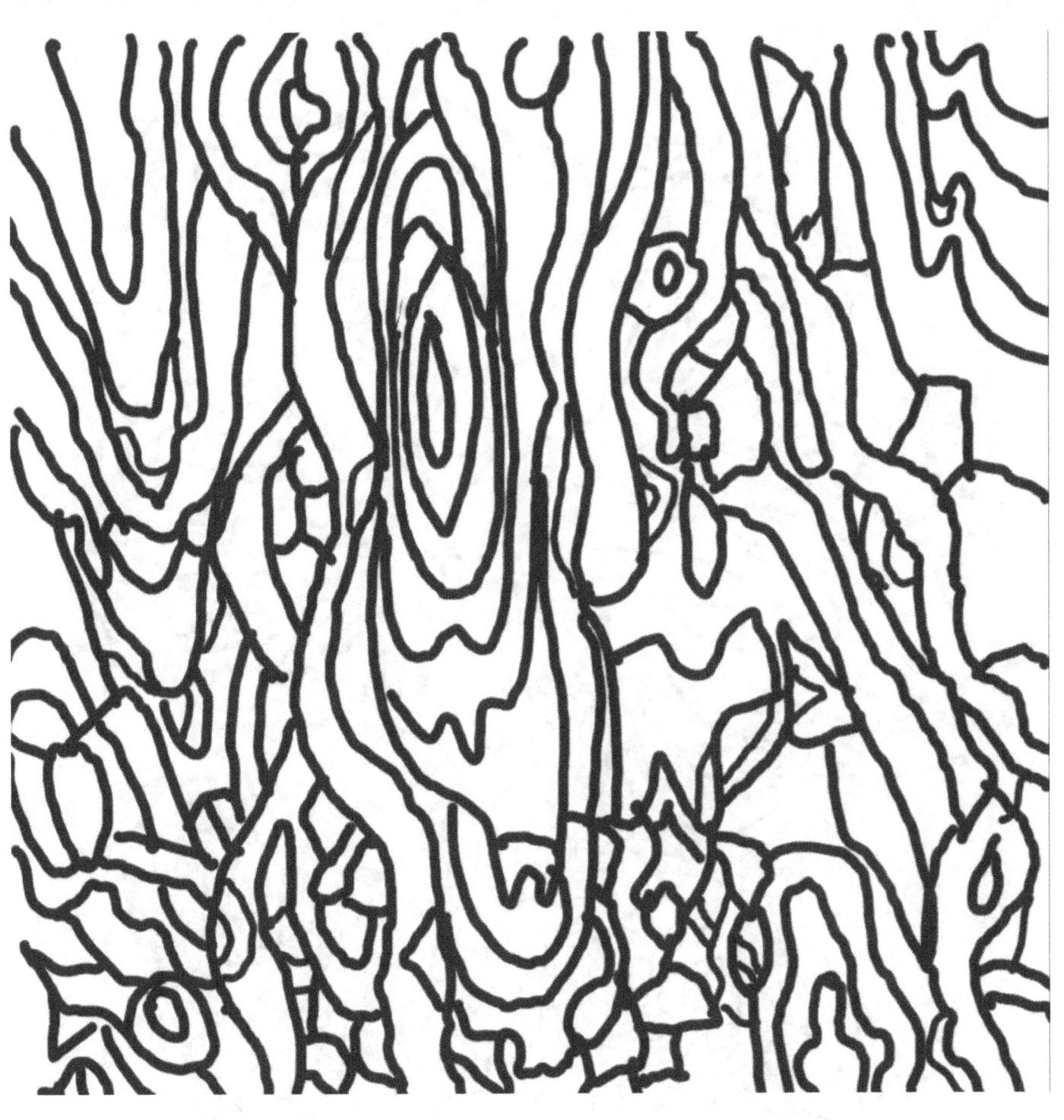

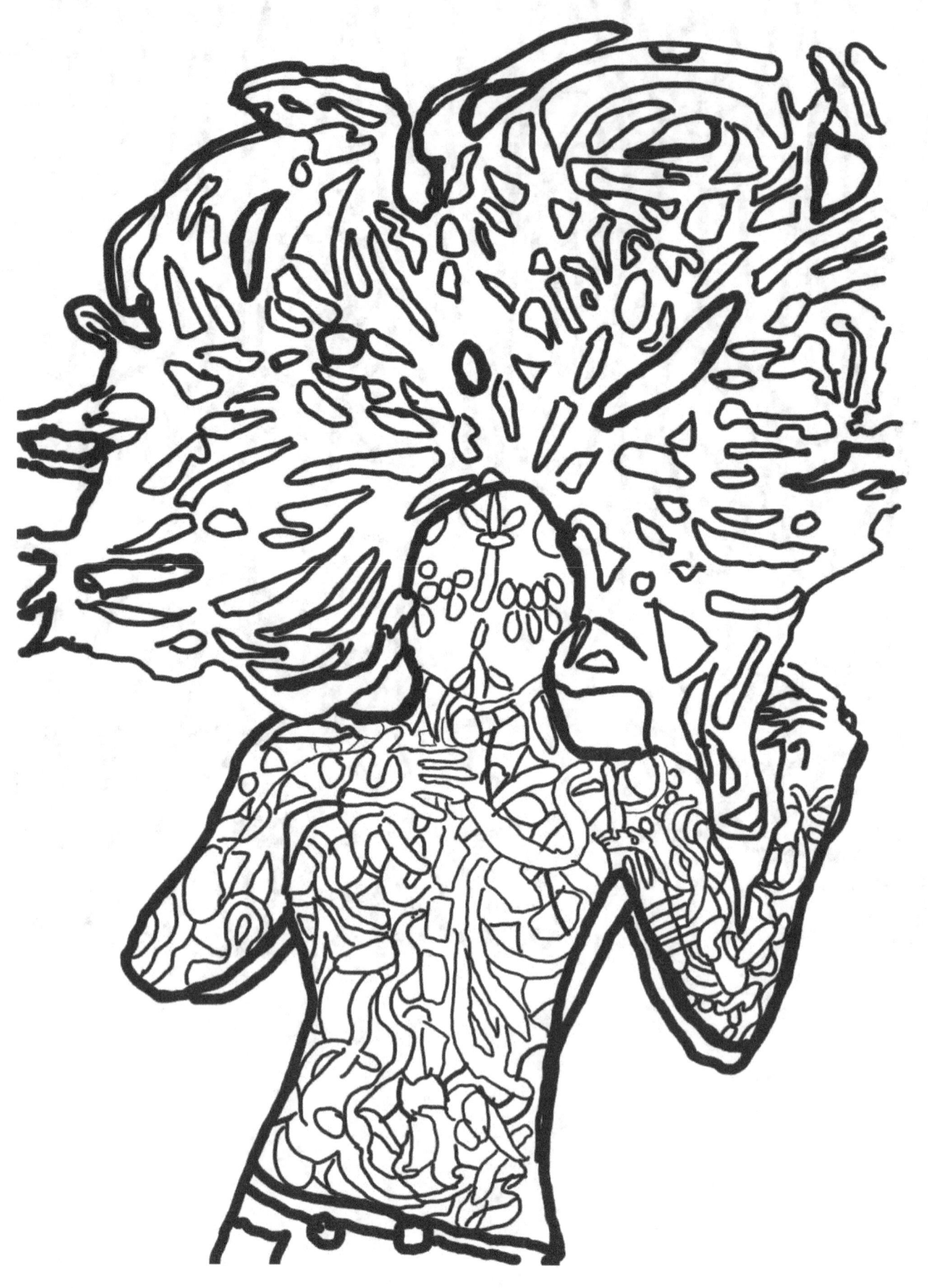

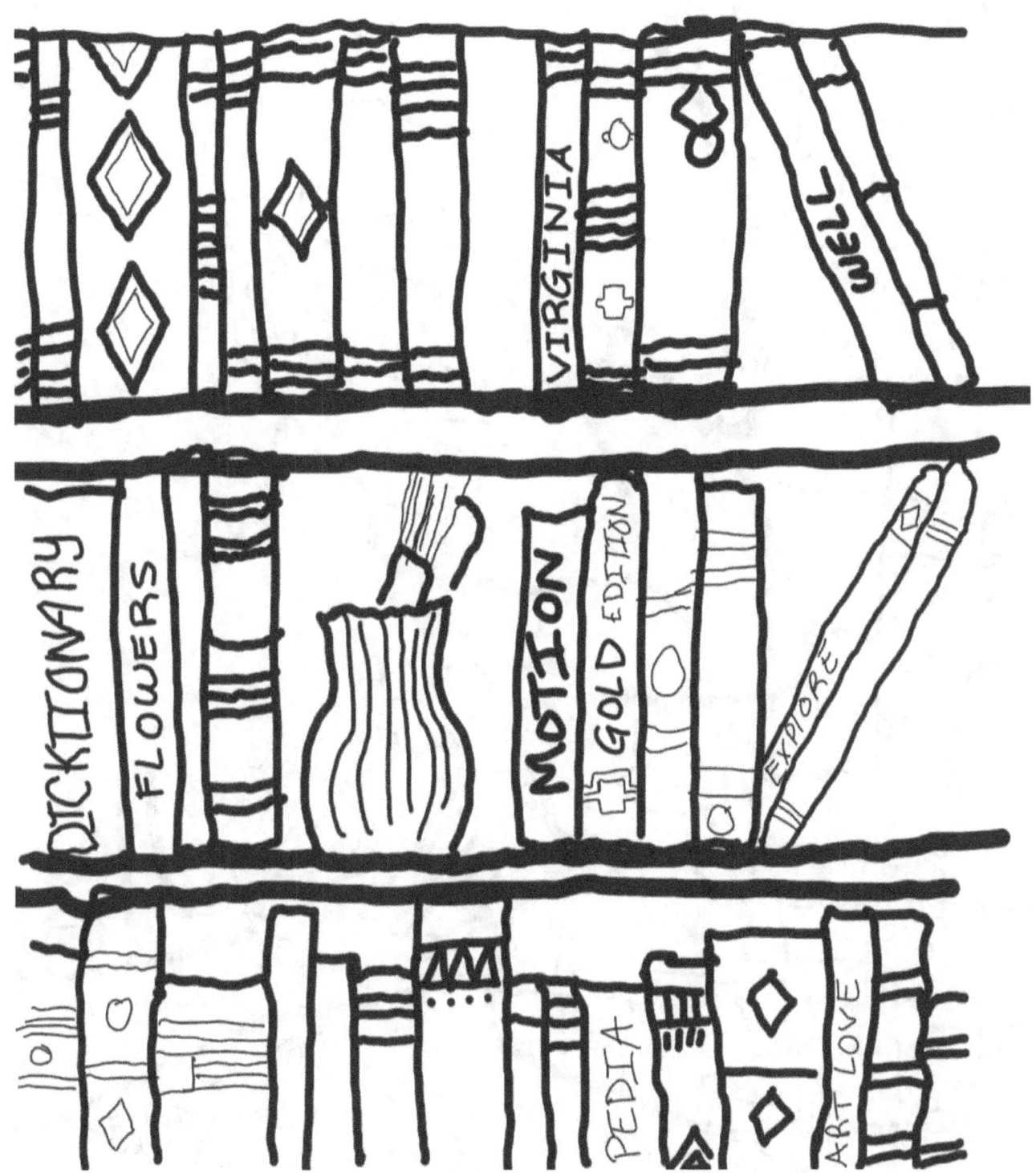

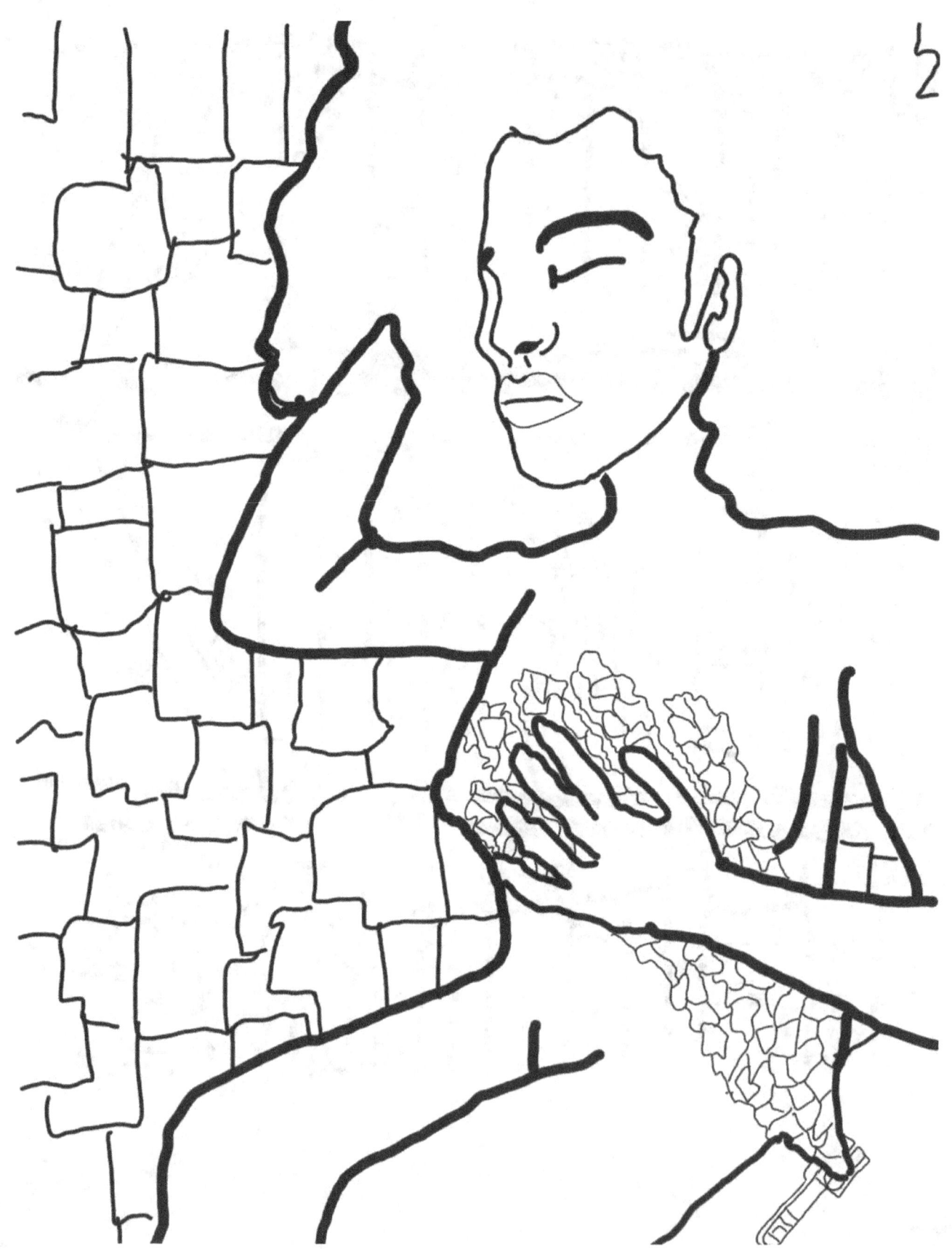

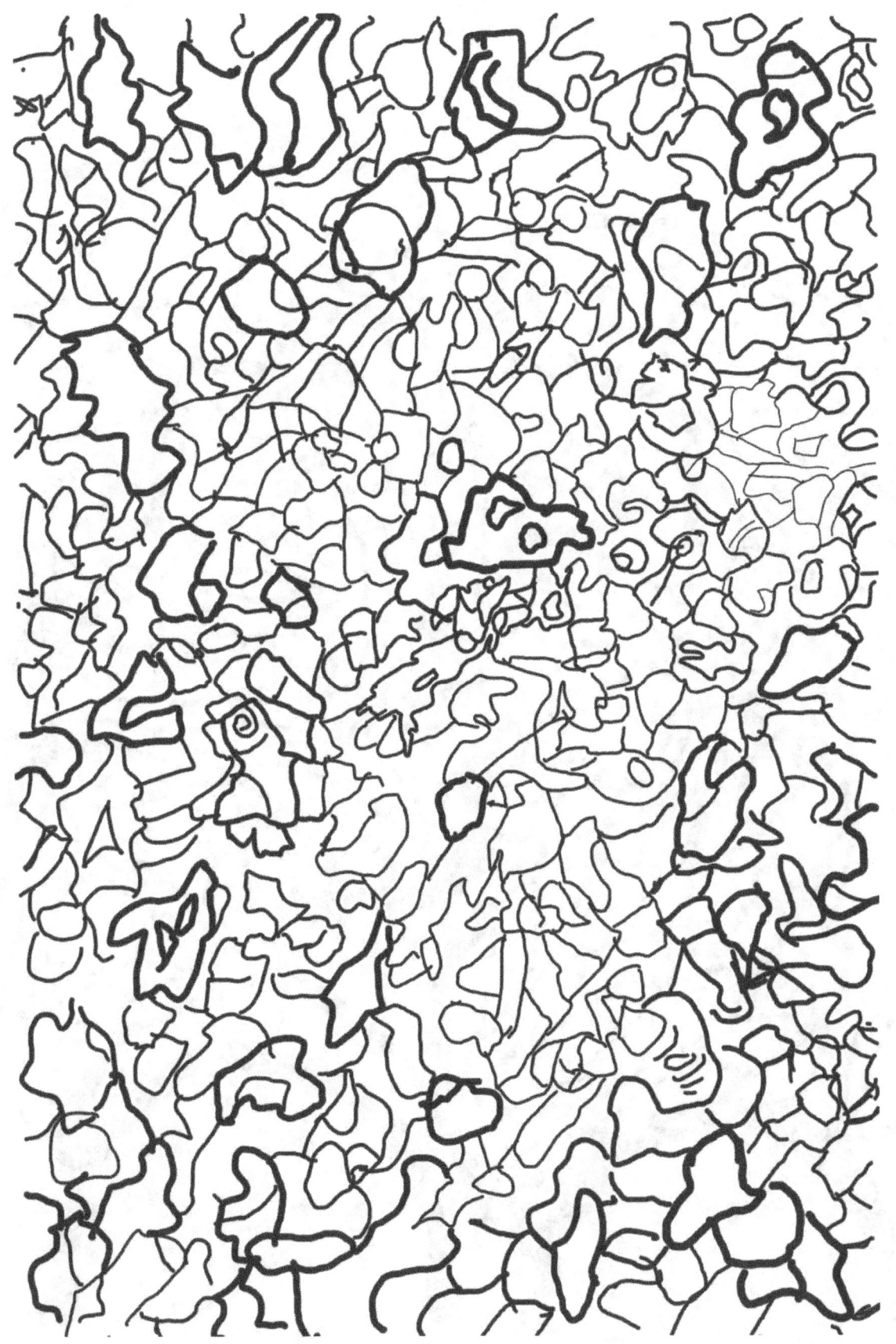

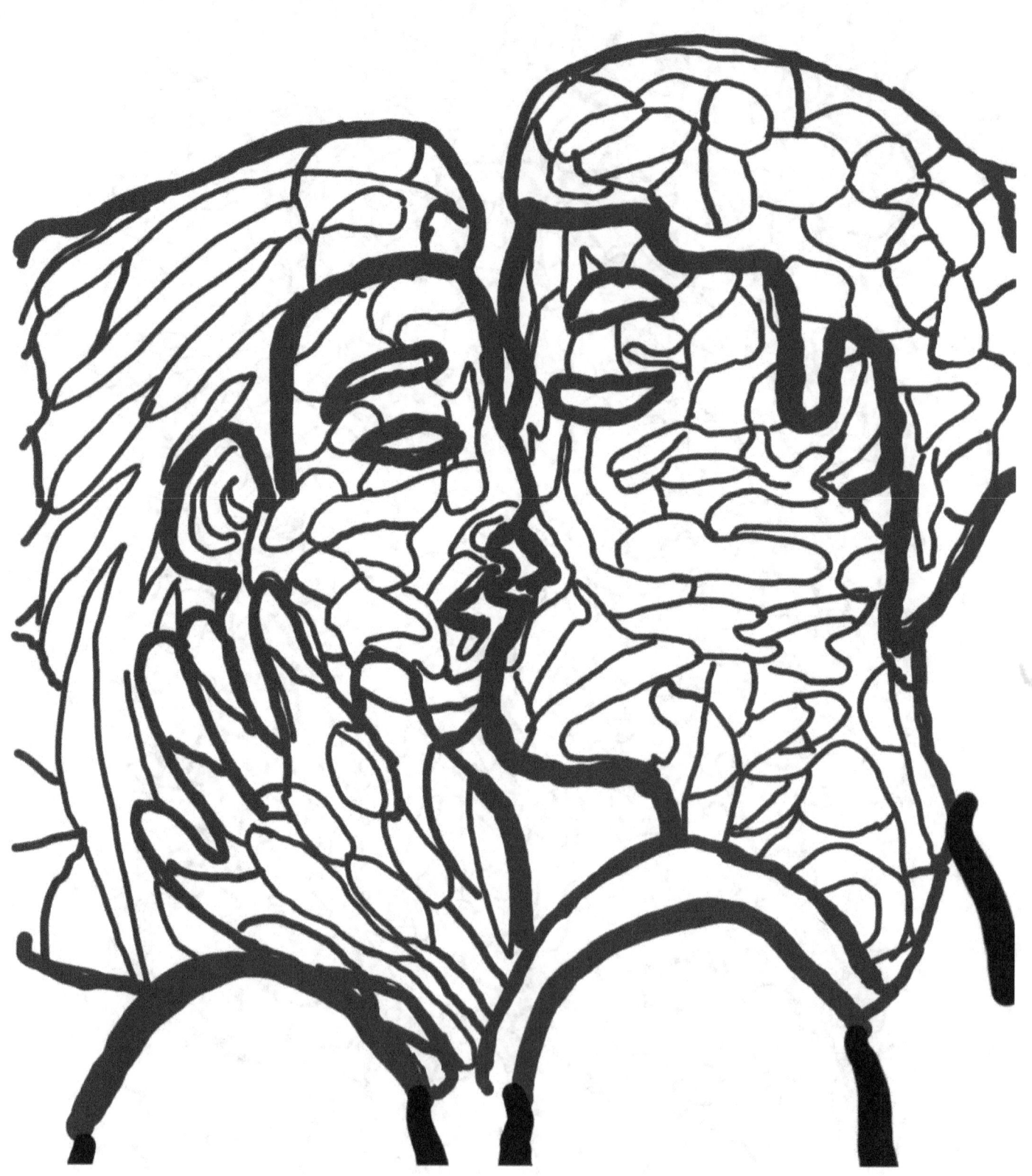

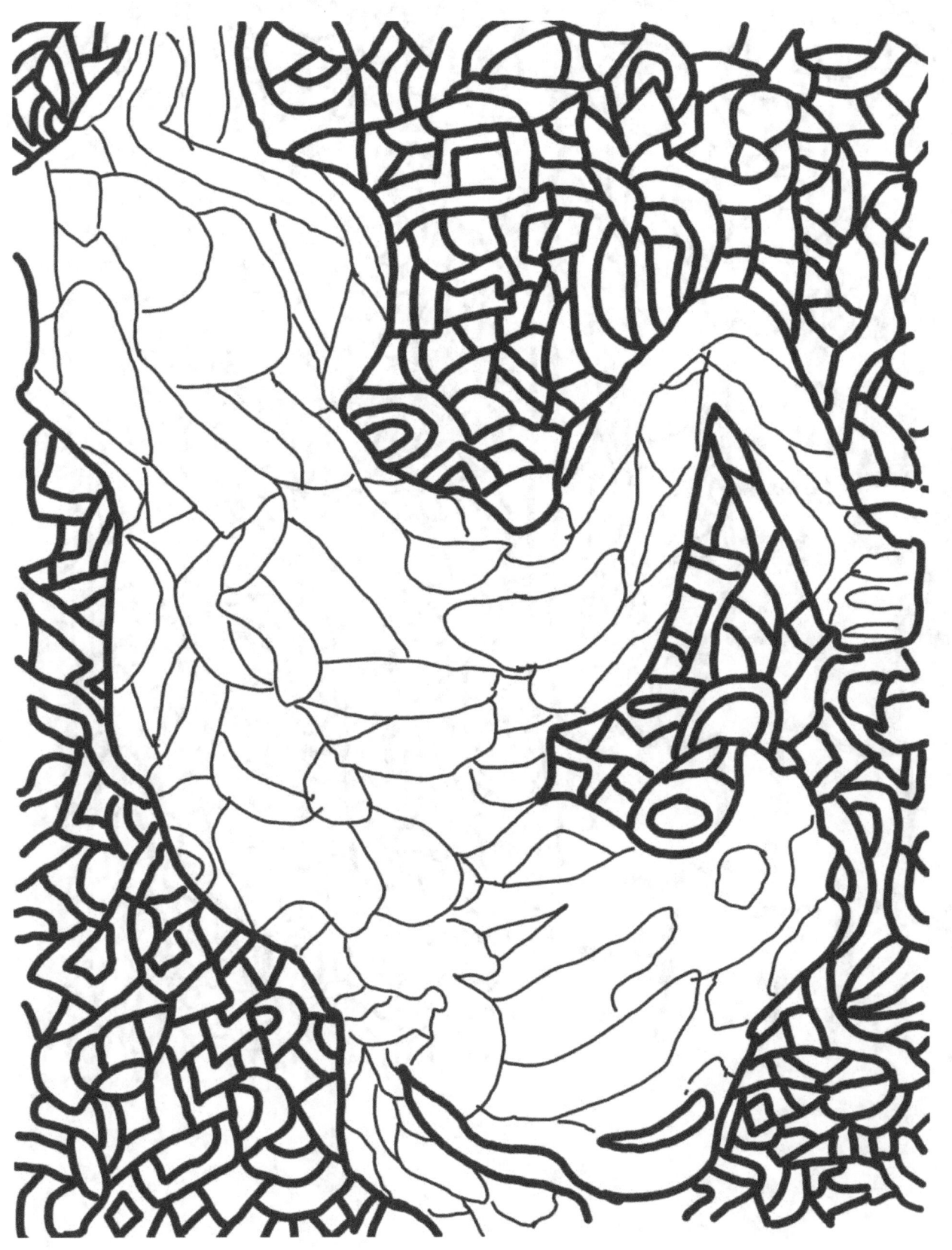

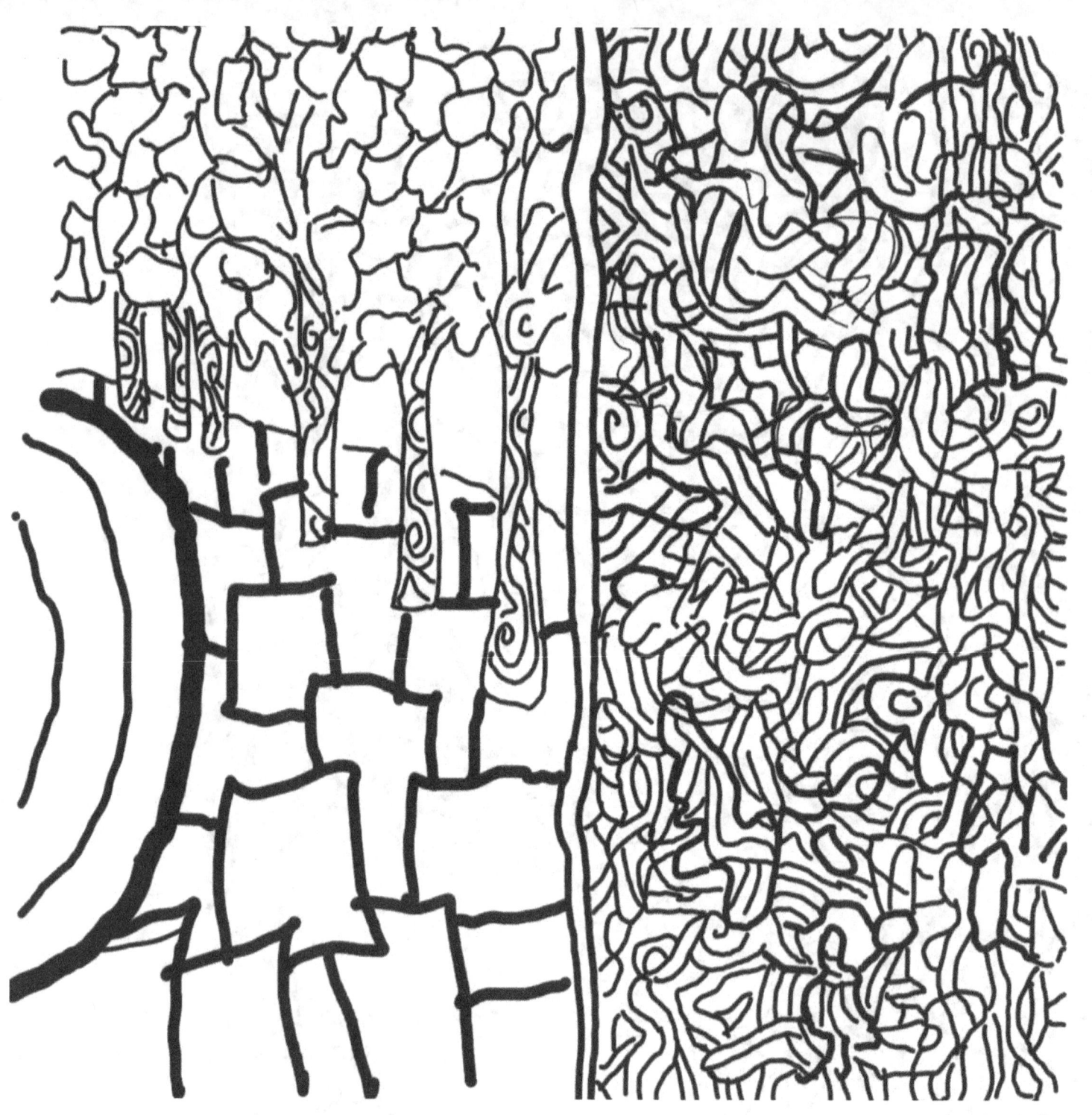